Canadian Biography Series

MORLEY CALLAGHAN:
LITERARY ANARCHIST

Morley Callaghan, "professional contrarian."

Morley Callaghan

LITERARY ANARCHIST

Gary Boire

ECW PRESS

Copyright © ECW PRESS, 1994

CANADIAN CATALOGUING IN PUBLICATION DATA
Boire, Gary A.
Morley Callaghan : literary anarchist

Includes bibliographical references.
ISBN 1-55022-185-X

1. Callaghan, Morley, 1903–1990 – Biography.
2. Novelists, Canadian (English) – 20th century –
Biography.*   I. Title.

PS8505.A43Z57 1994   C813'.52   C94-930592-8
PR9199.3.C35Z57 1994

This book has been published with the assistance of the Ministry of Culture,
Tourism and Recreation of the Province of Ontario, through funds provided
by the Ontario Publishing Centre, and with the assistance of grants from the
Department of Communications, The Canada Council, the Ontario Arts
Council, and the Government of Canada through the Canadian Studies
and Special Projects Directorate of the Department of the Secretary of State
of Canada. This book has also been published with the help of a grant from
the Canadian Federation for the Humanities, using funds provided by the
Social Sciences and Humanities Research Council of Canada.

Design and imaging by ECW Type & Art, Oakville, Ontario.
Printed by Imprimerie Gagné, Louiseville, Québec.

Distributed by General Distribution Services,
30 Lesmill Road, Don Mills, Ontario M3B 2T6.
(416) 445-3333, (800) 387-0172 (Canada), FAX (416) 445-5967.

Distributed to the trade in the United States exclusively
by InBook, 140 Commerce Street, P.O. Box 120261,
East Haven, Connecticut, U.S.A. 06512.
Customer service: (800) 243-0138, FAX (800) 334-3892.

Distributed in the United Kingdom by Bailey Distribution,
Learoyd Road, Mountfield Road Ind Est, New Romney, Kent, TW28 8XU.

Published by ECW PRESS,
2120 Queen Street East, Suite 200
Toronto, Ontario M4E 1E2.

ACKNOWLEDGEMENTS

In the research and writing of this biography, I incurred debts to many people and institutions; without their help this project would never have been completed. I am grateful especially to Wilfrid Laurier University for awarding me a book preparation grant to cover all of the financial expenses involved in the research, and for providing a course remission grant which gave me the necessary time and space for the writing. My thanks go especially to Dr. Barry McPherson and Noni Coleman of the Research Office at Wilfrid Laurier.

I received tremendous help from the staff of numerous archives and libraries who searched their collections for Callaghan materials on my behalf. In particular, I want to thank Ian ten Cate, archivist for the Law Society of Upper Canada, who clarified certain features of legal studies at Osgoode Hall during the 1920s; Anne Goddard, National Archives of Canada, for permission to use and quote from materials held in the E.K. Brown, Robert Weaver, Frank and Dorothy Flaherty, and John Gray collections; Apollonia Lang Steele, University of Calgary, for permission to consult Callaghan's letters held in their general archives; Charlotte Stewart, McMaster University, for permission to quote from materials held in the William Ready Division of Archives and Research Collections; and Wendy Watson, Thomas Fisher Rare Book Library, University of Toronto, for permission to consult materials held in their Earle Birney, W.A. Deacon, A.J.M. Smith, and Barry Callaghan collections. I am also grateful to Bernard Lutz of the National Film Board of Canada who located Callaghan's 1942 screenplay and his letters to John Grierson, and to Joan Pennefather, Government Film Commissioner, who gave me permission to quote from this material. The National Film Board holds the copyright of the screenplay. I also wish to acknowledge Macmillan Canada for permission to reprint excerpts from *That Summer in Paris*.

In the United States I want to thank Ron Chepesiuk, Head of Special Collections, Winthrop University, South Carolina, for permission to quote from materials held in their Nathan Asch Collection; Cynthia Fara, Harry Ransom Humanities Research Center, University of Texas at Austin, for permission to consult materials held in their Josephine Herbst and

John Herrmann Archives; Stephen Plotkin, John Fitzgerald Kennedy Library, for permission to quote from materials held in their Ernest Hemingway Collection; Patricia Willis, Yale Collection of American Literature, Beinecke Rare Book and Manuscript Library, Yale University, for permission to quote from materials held in the Yale Review Archives and the Ezra Pound Archive; and Margaret M. Sherry, Department of Rare Books and Special Collections, Princeton University Library, and Edith Golub of Charles Scribner's Sons, respectively, for permission to quote from materials held in the Charles Scribner's Publishing Archives held at Princeton.

I also want to thank the following for their permission to reproduce photographic materials held in their collections: the Toronto Transit Commission Archives, the Canadian Broadcasting Corporation Archives, Barry Callaghan, the *Toronto Star*, and the *Globe and Mail*.

On a more personal note, I wish to thank Brandon Conron and Carolyn Conron, who shared their generous hospitality and memories of Callaghan; Charlie Boire, who corrected a number of my errors regarding Callaghan's visits with Dink Carroll and the sports department of the old *Montreal Star*; Bill Burrill of the *Toronto Star*, who shared his research on Hemingway; Claire Rumin Wilkes for her personal impressions; and Norman Klenman, who sent me his reminiscences of filming *Now That April's Here*.

For their advice and critical support I owe yet two more in a long line of personal and professional debts to James King of McMaster University who, as always, provided unerring critical advice on biographical research; and to Jim Doyle of Wilfrid Laurier University who generously shared his biographical insights and allowed me to read his own manuscript of his Stephen Leacock biography. For her indefatigable curiosity I thank my excellent research assistant, Elaine Auerbach; and for her continual secretarial support (which often stretches beyond the call of duty), Joanne Buchan. For their unstinting criticism and patience I also want to thank Robert Lecker, Jack David, Holly Potter, and Cynthia Sugars of ECW PRESS.

Finally, I am most grateful of all to Barry Callaghan, who graciously shared his time and personal experiences with me. As Callaghan's literary executor, he has given permission to quote from the correspondence and unpublished materials. Without his advice and criticism this manuscript would have many more factual errors than it undoubtedly still has.

TABLE OF CONTENTS

LIST OF ILLUSTRATIONS

Morley Callaghan

LITERARY ANARCHIST

INTRODUCTION:
INVETERATE CONTRARIAN

At the time of his death on 25 August 1990, at the age of
eighty-seven, Morley Callaghan had had a long and eclectic
career. Not only was he the internationally known author of
over twenty novels and novellas, over two hundred journalistic
articles, and over a hundred short stories, but he had also been
and, in varying degrees remained, a student of law, an amateur
theologian, a journalist, businessman, husband, father, playwright, radio and television personality, sports columnist, and
social commentator. Throughout this "glorious career" (Callaghan, "There Are Gurus" 20), he remained to the end what
many of his friends have described as a professional contrarian,
an inveterate counterpuncher.

Callaghan was, as he himself might say, a rare bird: a rare,
exasperatingly playful, serious, Irish-Canadian, sceptical, devout,
ferocious, sensitive, talented, dialectical, curious, ironic, corny,
unsentimental, yet cantankerously aggressive, individualist. He
was a man who insisted always on the importance of seeing "the
world with [your] own eyes" (Callaghan, "Talk" 7). He was also
an extraordinarily warm, but demanding man who insisted on
being truly alert — on being aware of, and involved in, the world
that surrounded him. With Callaghan there was no room for
mediocrity; he lived the life of the mind and body with an almost

unrelenting relish. And he demanded no less of his friends and acquaintances.

In each of his many life roles, Callaghan was insistent on one thing: that we continually struggle with ideologies, with the unwritten official expectations that surround us. He believed that whenever one of these ideologies and expectations was internalized, people became essentially puritanical, virtually blinded to the real. Though it might seem odd now to think of the religious author of *Such Is My Beloved* as a subversive, carnivalesque clown, Morley Callaghan was just such an ever-changing, intellectual, and literary harlequin. Of course, his life was a series of contradictions. Callaghan justified his varied perceptions with the motto, "that was then, but this is now." His thought and practice were almost always sceptically dialectical; that is, his was a position of constantly shifting interrogations of any fixed intellectual, moral, or literary position.

As Callaghan himself remarked in 1985, he took an "anarchistic angle" on the world:

I think that the artist almost instinctively is an anarchist. Why is he an anarchist, although he may never work it out, programmatically or philosophically or anything? He's an anarchist in the sense that while he is an artist, he uses his own eyes. You see, no-one comes along to correct his vision. And fundamentalists, whether they be Marxian or Christian, are people who come along to correct your vision. I don't need that kind of obnoxious treatment. (Callaghan, Personal interview)

Anarchism, as an intellectual concept, might seem an odd label for a man who was a lifelong supporter of the Liberal party, but as a political strategy and literary attitude, it seems singularly appropriate to Callaghan's celebration of a fierce individualism.

Within the multiple folds of these ambiguities, what follows is a prefatory biography, a preamble to the major detailed life study that Morley Callaghan so richly deserves. My emphasis is deliberately placed on Callaghan's early years — his twenties, thirties, and forties — during which he made his first major contributions to world literature. Given the space limitations of this series, however, this biography represents an initial attempt to trace only some of the intellectual lineaments that made up his literary and personal anarchism, the "many-coloured" struggles of his multiple lives.

AN ANCIENT LINEAGE

Turn-of-the-century Toronto. Horses and buggies wind their way along Yonge Street, jostling for space with tramways and the odd, obtrusive motor car; gypsy families camp by the Humber River; hayfields grace Eglinton Avenue, just west of Yonge. The front page of the *Globe* for Monday, 23 February 1903 — one day after Morley Callaghan was born — reports that the morality department of Montreal considers the posters of one Mrs. Patrick Campbell immoral, and sports a dateline plastered across the top of her décolleté gown.

Black-and-white photographs; yellowing newspapers. This anecdote represents a now whimsical moment in Canada's puritan history. It points toward an ancient lineage, a world that for most readers in the 1990s appears strangely antiquated, the world into which Edward Morley Callaghan was born on Sunday, 22 February 1903. He was the second son of working-class, Irish-Canadian, Roman Catholic parents. In the overwhelmingly British, predominantly Protestant community of turn-of-the-century Toronto, the family thus belonged to a religious and ethnic minority. Irish Catholics formed only 15% of Toronto's British immigrant population by 1913 (Lemon 14). This "outsidedness" would texture Callaghan's life and written oeuvre.

Information about Callaghan's earliest years in Toronto is both limited and highly subjective. We have only his rare conversational remarks and few published comments to guide us. These, however, uniformly point to a closely knit, congenial

FIGURE 2

Turn-of-the-century Toronto: Yonge Street north from King (October, 1911).

family in which both parents provided a lively political and cultural atmosphere, one that especially fostered literary, musical, and Liberal-party activities.

The first Callaghan home was at 35 Woolfrey Avenue, within walking distance of the Protestant school, Withrow Public, on Bain Street, which Callaghan attended from 1909 until 1916. Roman Catholic schools were few and far between in Toronto. His mother, Mary Dewan, came from Collingwood, Ontario, where the young Callaghan would spend summer holidays with his mother's relatives (Conron, *Morley Callaghan* [1966] 19).

Unlike Ernest Hemingway's doting mother, who would keep a diary tracing her son's writerly aspirations and her own active encouragements, Mary Dewan was more quietly supportive of her sons' intellectual and artistic ambitions. She enjoyed reading poetry to her family, especially Edgar Allan Poe, for which Callaghan maintained a taste throughout his life. As he remarked in 1964, "Happily for me, and most influentially, my parents were of the generation that took to the English poets as the general public now takes to the most popular novelists. As a boy I could rhyme off hundreds of lines from Tennyson, Byron, Keats, Moore, Wordsworth, Kipling, without thinking of them as literature" ("An Ocean Away" 17). Mary's quiet cultivation of her sons wasn't based on a stay-at-home unworldliness; like her husband, Thomas, she was also active in Liberal-party causes, and it was she, in 1926, who excitedly told Morley over the telephone that his first story, "A Girl with Ambition," had been published in *This Quarter* (*That Summer* 50).

The Callaghans' older son, Burke, through formal musical training, developed into an exceptionally talented operatic singer who later performed at his brother's wedding. He was, moreover, regularly touted in the local papers as a promising star, but died suddenly in 1946 at the age of forty-four — during the "dark period" of Callaghan's life. Both boys were named after Irish patriots: Burke after Edmund Burke, "the champion of free trade with Ireland and of Catholic Emancipation," while Morley was named after John Morley, "biographer of Burke and twice chief secretary for Ireland in the Liberal government of William Gladstone" (Conron, *Morley Callaghan* [1966] 20).

This Irish connection came from Morley's father, Thomas Callaghan, an Irishman born in Wales who came to Canada in his youth as an indentured labourer, and worked initially for a doctor in Brantford, Ontario (Barry Callaghan, Personal interview). Later, he settled in Toronto where he became a dispatcher for the Canadian National Railway Express. Although in the early 1900s Toronto underwent a period of high unemployment and inflation, the family was, comparatively speaking, financially stable.

Given that Thomas and Mary named their sons after champions of the Irish cause, and that Thomas, too, was active on behalf of the Ontario Liberals, it seems fair to assume a family interest in both Canadian and Irish politics. In the mid-1960s Callaghan would remember his father, not only as a lover of popular music (though not jazz!), but also as a keen debater and ardent political worker in Toronto, activities supplemented by his contributions of satirical verse to two local newspapers, the *Telegram* and the *Moon*.

THAT IRISH SCEPTICISM

A flavour of the lively literary and political atmosphere of the Callaghan home can be gleaned from the *Moon*, a comic journal published in Toronto for a few years at the turn of the century. The paper specialized in satirical verse and prose, outrageous cartoons, and biting essays. Because it habitually identified its contributors pseudonymously or by initials only, it is impossible to ascribe with certainty any of the verse to Thomas Callaghan. But it is tempting, given his connections with the Liberal party, to link him with a poem, signed "T.C.," and published on 30 August 1902 (six months before Morley's birth).

"That Premier Majority — One" is a rollicking piece of doggerel that teasingly addresses the one-seat majority held by the Ontario Liberal government of George Washington Ross, and illustrates well the tone of unabashed sarcasm typical of the popular press at the time:

> Here's to you, Hon. Geo. Washington Ross,
> And your mammoth majority — ONE
> Let them say that it's all in your eye,
> That it's stolen from Dooley or Nye,
> Tories biased and small
> Couldn't see it at all,
> Tho' it stared at them thirty miles high, Sky-high,
> Only then through a glass of old rye.
> But, George (just between us), could you stand, say a "run"
> For a week on that huge multitudinous one?
> That cute little digit of one,
> That big, little trifle of one,
> That strange problematical,
> Globe autocratical,
> Grand old historical — ONE.

A more definite indicator of Thomas's open and supportive attitude towards his son's literary interests is recounted by Callaghan himself in *That Summer in Paris*. Reading through the copy of *This Quarter* that had published Callaghan alongside Joyce, Pound, Stein, and Hemingway, Thomas began chortling over an extract from Joyce's wildly surrealistic *Finnegans Wake*. Expecting a withering response about experimental prose, the young author petulantly demanded to know what was so funny: Thomas "looked up mildly . . . and he said with genuine pleasure, 'I think I understand this. Read it like Irish brogue. . . . It's like listening to someone talking in a broad Irish brogue, isn't it, Son?'" (*That Summer* 139).

As Callaghan grew up during this period of political struggle, his minority Irish-Catholic family was marked, not only by a love of literature, music, debate, and active social engagement, but also by a scepticism about the value of inherited or authorized explanations. As Barry Callaghan, Morley's son, has remarked,

Callaghan dinners were routinely occasions for argument and debate, during which Morley always "spoke in paragraphs" (Barry Callaghan, Personal interview). There, any idea — no matter how sacred — was up for dispute.

Callaghan's earliest, most formative years, then, were characterized by continued engagement with intellectual and social issues. It is not so much that he grew up during a time of social and philosophical transition (we all do), but that from his earliest days he was encouraged to approach those transitions from an independent — what he would later call an anarchistic — "angle." His struggle for an independent perspective gained particular momentum during Callaghan's high-school years at Riverdale Collegiate, the Protestant, public high school he attended from 1916 until 1921.

However, while Canada struggled into nationhood following the First World War, and as women finally won the vote in Canadian federal elections in 1918, the young Callaghan passed the violent early years of the roaring twenties in relatively idyllic ease. As a young boy he was most interested in athletics, an interest that would continue throughout his life. In high school he played hockey, football, and baseball, and pitched in the city's sandlot league at Christie Pits. And although his famous interest in boxing would develop later at the University of Toronto, in the early 1920s, he already aspired after a career as a professional athlete.

During the summers he had odd jobs, among these selling magazines while travelling through the Ottawa Valley by horse and buggy. He also worked part-time during the Christmas holidays for Simpsons on Yonge Street, selling neckties in the men's wear department. According to Brandon Conron, it was at this period that Callaghan began, however tentatively, to write short stories:

The summer before he entered the university he wrote three stories about a character named Old Mac who worked in Simpson's . . . and sold them to a Toronto magazine known as the *National Pictorial*. But it went bankrupt just before the stories were to be published, and Callaghan was not paid for his efforts. (*Morley Callaghan* [1966] 21)

EARLY INFLUENCES

Perhaps the most remarkable feature of Callaghan's formative years was his insatiable reading appetite, which spanned both North American and European writers. An extraordinarily rapid reader who would devour books by the boxload, he had the uncanny knack of being able to absorb both what was unquestionably canonized through tradition and what was just about to become mainstream literary fare. Even at this early period he read widely and critically.

As Stephen Leacock was publishing *Further Foolishness* in Canada in 1916, European and American literatures witnessed the disintegration of a flaccid Victorianism in the face of an emerging modernist experimentalism. While the last vestiges of Victorianism may have persisted in Samuel Butler's *The Way of All Flesh* and Henry James's *The Ambassadors* — both published in 1903 — James Joyce published one of Callaghan's favourite books, the revolutionary collection of stories, *Dubliners*, in 1914, and his *A Portrait of the Artist as a Young Man* in 1916. In 1920 there appeared two books that would later also profoundly influence the young Callaghan: Sinclair Lewis's *Main Street* and F. Scott Fitzgerald's *This Side of Paradise*.

Like George Orwell, Callaghan saw the stylistic developments of modernist techniques, not as an apolitical changeover to the merely new or trendy, but as the artist's self-conscious move away from mystified ideological imageries which sought an ideological moulding of the world. As he was to comment later in 1963: "Weren't the consequences of fraudulent pretending plain to anyone who would look around? Hadn't the great slogans of the first World War become ridiculous to me before I had left high school? Wilsonian idealism! Always the flight of fancy" (*That Summer* 20).

It was at Riverdale Collegiate that Callaghan began reading the American writers who would irrevocably change the face of modern literature and carve out the beginnings of a North American modernism. In his final year he stumbled upon the literary magazine *Smart Set*, a serendipitous moment that had far-reaching results. Edited by H.L. Mencken and George Jean Nathan (two of Callaghan's earliest favourite writers), *Smart Set* published such authors as George Moore, James Joyce, D.H. Lawrence, Ruth Suckow, Somerset Maugham, and Ford Madox Ford — writers who were meticulously dismantling Victorian conceptions of the novel. As Callaghan remarked of *Smart Set* to Robert Weaver, "I had this well of literature . . . laid at my feet when I was nineteen [sic]. What was going on in the world was suddenly brought very close to me . . . and I went for it" ("Talk" 5).

The author published in *Smart Set* who would most influence the young Callaghan was Sherwood Anderson, the man he later acknowledged as his literary father (Callaghan, "Talk" 15). From Anderson, Callaghan would learn the skills most precious for a young aspiring writer: a technique and set of themes, raw material for his own apprenticeship. Anderson, especially in *Winesburg, Ohio*, his collection of interrelated short stories, was able to depict the intensely symbolic within the limits of spare ironic description, thus representing the determining rhythms and alienating surges of the contemporary world. Callaghan's apprentice work, the Andersonian short stories of the late twenties that would later place him securely within the North American cultural pattern, wasn't long in the making.

FIRST PUBLICATION

In his final year at Riverdale — when he was only eighteen years old — Callaghan published his first journalistic story, "A Windy Corner at Yonge-Albert," in the Toronto *Star Weekly* on 6 August 1921. He was paid $12 for his efforts. The publication is of interest, not simply because it is Callaghan's first, but because it is thematically and stylistically characteristic of his writing during the twenties and thirties.

Like Anderson, Callaghan uses a confused narrator whose moral and, in this case, comic dilemma implicates the reader. As in the neocolonialist journalism of 1920s Toronto, the style encompasses mixed forms — both hard-boiled American ironies and British preciousness. We also see in this story Callaghan's early infatuation with ideas.

The plot is unnervingly simple: Callaghan's first-person narrator strolls up Yonge Street on a Sunday evening in search of "embryo orators." At the corner of Yonge and Albert, three "windy" speakers — a Bolshevik, a Socialist, and a Christian — contend for the crowd's attention. As the speeches proceed, the narrator (and by implication the reader) is suddenly stricken with uncertainty:

> Where shall we set our weary feet? . . . We are somewhat confused, a trifle dizzy, and inclined to be rather offended . . . but the spirit of compromise prevails and draws us to the human magnet in the centre. (17)

What makes Callaghan's short descriptive article so important is not simply its historical topicality and autobiographical grounding, but the fact that elements of the story would later appear and reappear in his mature fiction. That is, Callaghan's comic portrayal outlines what later developed into a profound, but cautious, fascination with revolutionary politics. As he remarked in 1985,

> I knew all the communists in town. And I tried very hard to be friendly with them. But you see, you always knew you were going to be used whatever happened; you were going to be used because they were like Christian and fundamentalist evangelists. Everything must serve the truth, or their truth, you see. And if they could use me to serve the truth, or their truth, it didn't matter a damn what I thought. (Personal interview)

This piece of high-school juvenilia also provides a wealth of information concerning Callaghan's earliest development as a writer. Despite its stylistic roughness, self-consciousness, and bumbling purple prose, his youthful article contains those features that would come to characterize his greatest fictions. Stylistically, it is typical of Callaghan's postcolonial hybridity, a style of writing where echoes of Shakespeare jostle with hard-boiled American humour; it shows him already drawing on local landscapes; it is decidedly journalistic and both socially and politically oriented; and it is noteworthy for its ability (albeit amateurish) to draw the reader into a dramatized moral dilemma. Thematically, the piece is remarkable for its dramatization of the essential conflicts that would confront virtually all of Callaghan's major characters up until 1948 — the moral and political problems of Marxism, Christianity, and Naturalism. Callaghan would later recycle the piece in some of his strongest novels where, interestingly, protagonists such as Father Stephen Dowling in *Such Is My Beloved*, or Michael Aikenhead in *They Shall Inherit the Earth*, engage in similar debates with Christian and Communist characters.

Before all of that, however, Callaghan would have to finish high school, attend university, study law at Osgoode Hall, and get married. He would have to visit New York and meet his American compeers. He would also have to get on in his first important job, at Toronto's brash and abrasive *Daily Star*. Here he would not only hone his famous reportorial style, but he would also contend with the greatest *bête noire* of his writing career: Ernest Hemingway.

GETTING ON IN THE WORLD

From 1921 until 1928 Callaghan experienced the first of his many crucial "conversions." During these years, British Toronto was growing very slowly towards multiculturalism. As Ernest Hemingway remarked in letters to friends in 1923, "I hate to leave Paris for Toronto the City of Churches" (Baker, *Selected Letters* 84). "In Toronto," he wrote to William Horne, "85% of the inmates attend a protestant church on Sunday. Official figures" (88). More blunt was his remark about Canada to Ezra Pound, "There is no doubt about it being the fistulated asshole of the father of seven among Nations" (*Selected Letters* 95).

In this puritan ambience, not only did Callaghan begin university-level studies and work vaguely toward a career in law, but he also began what would become a lifelong sporadic involvement with journalism. In 1923, especially, he experienced what were perhaps his first major transitions: he published his first journalistic pieces, began to write what would become his earliest published short stories, and became friends with Ernest Hemingway.

Most importantly, in 1924 Callaghan met his future wife, Loretto Florence Dee, at a college dance in Toronto. Originally from Collingwood, Ontario, Loretto was the daughter of Catherine Hamlin and Joseph Dee (with whom Morley and Loretto lived briefly after their return from Paris in 1929). Loretto was an art student at the University of Toronto during the early twenties. An intensely private woman with strong independent tastes in both literature and painting, Loretto consistently chose to avoid the glare of publicity and to work within the domestic sphere. By agreement with Morley, she later took primary responsibility in rearing their two sons, and introduced them to the arts of poetry, painting, and music. Though Morley would always be obstinate in the matter of revisions, Loretto became, in time, his first reader, whose opinions and comments he valued. Often, in fact, Morley would freely adapt Loretto's experiences or anecdotes into his short stories. ("The Red Hat," for example, was inspired by Loretto.) Throughout their life together, she and Morley would share a mutual devotion. Loretto married Morley on 16 April 1929 and remained his partner for fifty-five years until her death in 1984.

These principal, and overlapping, experiences make a purely chronological account of this period pointless, if not downright impossible. From this point on, we must look at Callaghan's life facet by facet, in relation to dominant themes or issues directly relevant to his writerly development, most notably his university experiences, his work at the *Star*, his registration at Osgoode Hall, and his founding of the Viking Lending Library.

VARSITY YEARS

In the autumn of 1921 Callaghan registered as a day scholar (a nonresident student) in the general arts programme of St. Michael's College at the University of Toronto. During the twenties, St. Mike's — a series of "old gray brick buildings with the primly Gothic touch" (Callaghan, *Varsity Story* 123) — was self-consciously the Catholic college of the university. It had its own set of rituals and protocols, and "[f]or some years previously," residents debated whether "the college should develop its own cultural pattern within its own walls," or if "the students might be enriched if blended more with the student life of the University as a whole" (*Varsity Story* 123). The rebellious Callaghan opted for the latter.

While attending St. Michael's, he took a relatively unconventional combination of courses, studying mainly English, French, philosophy, economics, and geology. He became a member of the Historical Club, which was "a selective club for chosen men from the various colleges to discuss the affairs of the day" (Callaghan, *Varsity Story* 113); he also joined the Literary Club whose entries he would write for the college yearbook in 1923 and 1924.

"[N]ot overweight then," he was a stocky five-foot-eight, "with dark brown curly hair and blue eyes," an athletic student who was already "fast with [his] tongue and, under pressure, fast with [his] fists" (*That Summer* 13). Not surprisingly, he concentrated on developing his debating skills — travelling to Pittsburgh in 1924 with the university team — boxing, and playing football, baseball, and hockey.

In the twenties Callaghan's general arts degree was despised by professors, upperclassmen, and Honours students alike. Seen as an easy option, the course was generally perceived as "[f]our years of beautiful bumming" (Callaghan, *Varsity Story* 91). But Callaghan was hardly a loafer. He spent his time reading fiction and journalism voraciously, developing, however embryonically, what would later become a consuming interest in political radicalism, fascism, scientific determinism, and Christian theology. Now, most notably, he began to read the works of Christian theologian Jacques Maritain, whose seminal *Éléments de philosophie* started to appear in 1923, as well as St. Thomas Aquinas. The metaphysics of both philosophers, Callaghan later recalled, "were to be treated with grudging suspicion" (*That Summer* 20).

Years later, in 1948, he would write *The Varsity Story* as a fund-raising "novel" for the University of Toronto, donating all of the royalties to the university's development fund. The book is a thinly disguised autobiography in which virtually every major character tries "stubbornly to create a little design from isolated bits of knowledge" (*Varsity Story* 76). Most interesting is the autobiographical character of Tom Lane, who is not only physically and intellectually similar to Callaghan, but who becomes the main vehicle through which Callaghan discloses critical features of his own self-image.

As *The Varsity Story* unfolds, the drama of Tom Lane reenacts what was Callaghan's own growing ambition to be a writer, grounded not in a colonial mentality, but in the here and now of contemporary Canada. As Tom defends his decisions to study widely and read independently, his words uncannily echo and anticipate Callaghan's own artistic and nationalist sentiments over the years. Lane decides to become a writer in Toronto rather than a student in England, and remarks to Arthur Tyndall, who is himself a transplanted colonial from New Zealand,

". . . a man should sometimes look around, see things freshly. I mean with his own eyes. I don't want to get trained to see the world through somebody else's eyes. . . . I don't want to be just a ghoul. . . . [l]iving only in the minds of dead men. . . . All a writer has, if he is any good . . . is his own eyes and his own ears. . . . I see things the way I do because I grew up around here. It's all I have, but it's mine. If I keep it I'll at least be trying to look at the world in my own way." (93, 114–15)

Callaghan admits to having read "wildly" during his university years: "Dostoevski, Joseph Conrad, Sinclair Lewis, Flaubert; *The Dial, The Adelphi,* and the old *Smart Set* . . . ; Catherine [sic] Mansfield. D.H. Lawrence — everything" (*That Summer* 13–14). Everything — including the writers who would later exert tremendous influence on him (whether or not he enjoyed them) and who were now beginning to publish the monumental books of the early twentieth century. These included Eliot's *The Waste Land,* Joyce's *Ulysses,* and Lewis's *Babbit,* all appearing in 1922; André Breton's *Manifeste du surrealism* (which Callaghan despised) and Hemingway's *In Our Time* (which he admired), both published in 1924; and, in 1925, Dreiser's *An American Tragedy* and Fitzgerald's *The Great Gatsby,* which set the tone of much subsequent American writing.

During his varsity years Callaghan "was experiencing a kind of elation he might never know again. . . . [an] ascendancy of the mind giving him a free unlimited joy that he wanted to keep in his heart wherever he went" (Callaghan, *Varsity Story* 97). What is most intriguing is the fact that he retained this exultation, this joyful renaissance scope. To Callaghan, university meant the opening of intellectual and emotional horizons; it also offered the space in which he would grow as both a man and a writer.

REPORTING FOR THE *STAR*

Throughout his life Callaghan was fascinated by serendipitous experiences. As he remarked in a 1985 interview for CTV's *Lifetime,* "Has it ever occurred to you how your whole life can change almost accidentally? Our lives are so dependent on a trifling circumstance." During the summer of 1923, before entering his third year of university, Callaghan's youthful career changed dramatically because of two "trifling circumstances": a sore arm and the boredom of Ernest Hemingway.

During the summer of 1923, Callaghan was obsessed with baseball. He had played for years in the university sandlot leagues at Christie Pits, and in 1923, with his brother Burke as catcher, played in the midget league, hoping to become a pitcher on one of the city's senior teams. The Callaghan brothers were hardly exceptional: Torontonians in the twenties conducted a love affair with their ball teams, surpassing even the present-day infatuation with the Blue Jays.

At the same time, Callaghan began summer work as a general labourer in the Laidlaw lumberyard in Toronto, " 'slugging' lumber," like Harry Trotter in *Strange Fugitive*, "with five husky immigrant laborers" (*That Summer* 13). The work horrified him and was virtually disastrous: the heavy labour strained his pitching arm to the point of numbness. To save his arm he sought out less strenuous work and, following the example of his boyhood friend Art Kent, wrangled his way onto the summer staff of the Toronto *Star*. As Callaghan remarked in the *Lifetime* interview, "with all the audacity of youth" he talked his way past the city editor, Harry Johnston, by exaggerating his limited experience on the *Varsity* newspaper. Lying through his teeth about both his experience and ability — he had never before been in a newsroom! — Callaghan was hired. He would work at the paper for the next three summers — and for three afternoons a week during term — starting at $20 a week.

Callaghan's experience with the *Star* constitutes an extraordinarily complex phase in his intellectual and artistic development. Quite simply, he had now come into firsthand contact with the turbulence of human experience. In the beginning he rewrote obituaries and covered such mundane assignments as druggists' conventions in downtown Toronto; later he covered the hotel beat, the courts, political meetings, isolated disasters, and human tragedies. Occasionally he would revert, however reluctantly, to journalists' tricks to exact information, once with-holding the truth about a young girl's death to obtain a photograph from the distraught family. "I hated myself," he said of the episode later (*That Summer* 43). Callaghan ran the full gamut of a junior reporter's duties, an experience from which he gained an increased awareness of human complexity.

While at the *Star*, Callaghan began to consolidate his characteristically intransigent attitudes. He often ran afoul of the paper's tyrannical editor, Harry Hindmarsh, whom Hemingway felt was "neither a just man, a wise man, nor a very honest man" (Baker, *Selected Letters* 109). Callaghan was in fact fired five times by Hindmarsh for his insubordinate, "wise-guy" attitude. He argued about contemporary writing with his colleagues, most of whom (including the popular writer Greg Clark) favoured conservative prose in contrast to Callaghan's preference for literary experimentalism. With Hemingway's friend Jimmy Cowan, the other person at the *Star* who shared Callaghan's tastes, he defended Hemingway against sniping office mates and unfriendly reviewers. As Callaghan ironically remarked in the 1985 *Lifetime* interview, despite the fact that "I am the kindliest, most reasonable, rational man and the easiest guy in the world to get along with . . . I presented the whole problem of the university man."

As a junior reporter Callaghan did not merit the luxury of his own byline; however, two stories that can be attributed to him with confidence are "Radical 'Bill' Foster Urges Labor Revolt" and "Wipe Out Craft Unionism, States 'Most Dangerous Red' " — both published on 7 August 1923. The articles concern the illegal visit to Canada of William Z. Foster, founder of the Trade Union Educational League and later national secretary of the Communist Party of America. Both stories have their fair share of "red-bashing" and reveal Callaghan's *status quo* aversion to communism; but, interestingly, both offset this conservative line by riskily stressing Foster's admirable individuality, his vital antagonism toward all forms of oppression.

Stylistically, both pieces are remarkable for their telling detail, searching dialogue, and ironic understatement. Callaghan takes time, for example, to remark that Foster is a "blue-eyed fellow" in a brown suit who looks "as if he had merely the ambitions of a street car conductor" ("Wipe Out Craft Unionism"). As his question-and-answer format outlines Foster's revolutionary programme, he communicates the kernel of the story, an approach he would later develop in his portraits of such communists as Isaac Pimblett in *Strange Fugitive* or Charlie Stewart in *Such Is My Beloved*. Described as a "radical among radicals," Foster emerges overall as a strongly committed, complex figure whose attitudes bear "a singular resemblance to the attitude of an individualist." Neither of Callaghan's articles is an example of brilliant journalism; both, however, reveal his earliest working out of a literary-journalistic style.

Forced to learn the idiom of "hard cold news" (*That Summer* 16), which included fitting words to things with a minimum of elaboration, Callaghan was also developing an imagistic prose style, a style that was now beginning to evolve in his earliest stories. The *Star* had given Callaghan the time and space in which to perfect his art, providing him with a number of crucial experiences: an engagement with the working world (with all of its turbulence and complexity); training in the craft of writing; and the opportunity to wed practice with theory. It also gave him his first contact with "a dedicated artist": Ernest Hemingway (*That Summer* 30).

ERNEST HEMINGWAY

Though Callaghan's relationship with Hemingway was fraught with paradoxes and complications, the facts surrounding their initial meeting are relatively simple. Four years Callaghan's senior, Hemingway had published his first book, *Three Stories and Ten Poems*, earlier in 1923 and now enjoyed a certain prestigious notoriety among *Star* staffers. Having worked off and on for the paper since 1920, most recently as its European correspondent in Paris, he returned to Toronto in the autumn of 1923 with his wife,

FIGURE 3

Callaghan the exile, in 1929.

Hadley, so their child could be born on North American soil. Hemingway began work as a local reporter on 10 September 1923, and almost immediately felt chafed under the editorship of Harry Hindmarsh who regularly burdened him with mundane assignments.

In *That Summer in Paris* Callaghan outlines his initial meeting with Hemingway. Writing an article in the *Star* library in the autumn of 1923, Callaghan glanced up to see Hemingway watching him, obviously killing time and looking for someone to talk to (27–28). The young reporters felt an immediate rapport and in the following weeks often met to discuss writing (notably Fitzgerald), read one another's fiction, and share opinions. One day that autumn, as Callaghan was perusing the proofs of *In Our Time*, Hemingway read one of Callaghan's manuscripts — which one is uncertain — and remarked, " 'You're a real writer. You write big-time stuff. All you have to do is keep on writing' " (*That Summer* 29).

The friendship continued after Hemingway resigned from the *Star* in disgust with Hindmarsh on 1 January 1924, after only four months in Toronto. When he left for Paris on 12 January, he autographed a copy of *Three Stories and Ten Poems* for Callaghan and promised to circulate his stories among the European literary magazines. Callaghan was delighted: he had made friends with "a great writer" who now offered to help him publish his stories (*That Summer* 26). Their friendship over the next six years — particularly in Paris during the summer of 1929 — was not, however, an uncomplicated delight. The contorted mix of personal and writerly needs — Hemingway's need to play the superior writer, Callaghan's shifting need to be first disciple, then master in his own right — would constitute a fascinating, complex, and moving literary friendship, one that would initially not only provide the younger Callaghan with some beneficial writerly support, but that would ultimately involve a series of emotional contortions and personal disappointments for both men.

To begin with, the two writers conducted a hearty literary correspondence. Callaghan's surviving ten letters, written occasionally on Press Gallery letterhead, reveal a joking, youthful enthusiasm, coupled with a brisk hardheaded interest in the mechanics of writing and publishing. He often asked for Hemingway's honest opinion — but rarely his advice — limiting questions to queries like "Are these stories good enough to be recommended by you to some publisher. . . . Do they need a good deal of editing? or would they not do in any event?" (Letter to Hemingway, [Autumn 1925]). Callaghan's letters, in fact, are very much those of a joyfully enthusiastic younger writer in love with writing, asking an older, published, and congenial friend for his opinions.

In his letters to Hemingway, Callaghan also expresses a pragmatic concern with the cold practicalities of getting published. He wonders whether a Canadian writer can publish internationally if he uses Canadian settings; he despairs of Canadian tastes for the romantic and sentimental. Throughout, he is incorrigibly humorous, indulging in playful gossip about the Toronto *Star*, off-colour religious and sexual jokes, and an overall youthful enthusiasm for the art of writing prose. He also includes factual news, such as the repeal of the Ontario Temperance Act in 1926; as Morley remarks to "Dear Hem," "If you were here we could walk sternly and deliberately into an hotel, blow froth off the beer, and discuss the evolution of the modern short story" (29 April [1926]). Callaghan's topics range widely and include personal news, theological conundrums, and jibes at Canadian claptrap literary tastes.

SET ON PUBLISHING

Most interesting is the information these letters provide concerning Callaghan's astonishingly prolific writing activities from 1923 to 1926: how things quickly began to fall into place for him; how, during these years, he evolved a clear and distinctive aesthetic credo; and how the complexly intersecting nature of his friendship with Hemingway developed and then began, ever so subtly, to fade.

Callaghan's interest in deflating literary pomposity is most evident in the stories and early novella he included with these letters. He had begun drafting stories in the summer of 1923, later showing Hemingway a long story of between 10,000 and 15,000 words dealing with a young man's first sexual affair. By October 1925 — a full year before his first published short story and just following his graduation from university — Callaghan mailed ten stories to Hemingway, including the long one he called "Along with Youth" (a title borrowed from one of Hemingway's poems). Four of these would be published by 1927: "A Girl with Ambition" (*This Quarter*, 1925–26), "Amuck in the Bush" (*The American Caravan*, 1927), "A Wedding Dress" (*This Quarter*, 1927), and "Last Spring They Came Over" (*transition*, 1927). While four of the ten stories would remain unpublished — the lengthy "Along with Youth," as well as "I Should Have Been a Preacher," "On the Way Home," and "Things" — they all bear the mark of Callaghan's interest in cold hard realism, and, given the temper of the times, his frank treatment of sexual desire, pregnancy, and rape were as controversial as Hemingway's blunt stories "Up in Michigan" and "Soldier's Home," both of which Callaghan admired.

By the end of 1925, while he was articling as a law student, Callaghan had also written what he considered to be his first novel, "An Autumn Penitent," which he posted to Hemingway on 1 December 1925. By April 1926, Callaghan wrote that he had rewritten some of the stories he'd originally sent to Hemingway, including "Along with Youth," and had sent them with three new stories to Edward O'Brien, editor of the annual *The Best Short Stories*. O'Brien subsequently offered to act as Callaghan's British agent.

All told, in the three years from the summer of 1923 until the spring of 1926, during his early twenties, Callaghan wrote thirteen stories and one short novel. Despite his complaints about writer's block over the next year, by 8 March 1927 he had told Hemingway about five more new stories and asserted that he was "well into" *Strange Fugitive* (which as yet remained untitled).

All of these grim, pared-down stories, with their unorthodox subject matter and crisp reportorial prose, corroborate Callaghan's claim in *That Summer in Paris* that it was during the early twenties that he evolved his artistic credo: "Orthodoxy was for fat comfortable inert people who agreed to pretend, agreed to accept the general fraud, the escape into metaphor" (*That Summer* 20). As he remarked ironically to Hemingway, "Do you think my stories are too bare? Should there be more similes in the name of BEAUTY?" (Letter to Hemingway, 11 Oct. [1925]). The joking comment must have delighted Hemingway, for both men, following in the steps of Anderson and Dreiser, had begun to challenge what they considered the ornate embroideries of existing literature; both shared a dedication to such imagist ideals as the use of everyday language and rhythms, and the artist's rejection of audience expectation in favour of his or her own vision.

Callaghan's opinion of Hemingway's writing was uniformly positive. In a letter of 7 November 1926, Callaghan remarks of *The Sun Also Rises*, "Ah Master, I just read your novel. I make furrows with my nose in the dust. I lay in bed this morning for an hour feeling how good it was." However, his impressions were nonetheless highly independent. A case in point involved Hemingway's 1926 *The Torrents of Spring*, a ferocious parody of one of Callaghan's favourite works, Sherwood Anderson's *Dark Laughter*. Callaghan wrote to praise Hemingway's "wallop at affectation," but said frankly, "I was depressed because you were so lustily kicking the props from under some good 'writing fellows.' Don't you think *Dark Laughter* a hell of a fine thing? I do" (Letter to Hemingway, 25 June [1926]). While Callaghan, understandably, was being diplomatic, he was hardly sycophantic.

This tension between independence and solidarity played continually throughout the Callaghan-Hemingway friendship, throughout the give-and-take of their camaraderie. The letters clearly show that Hemingway was supportive, but only to a point. Callaghan recognized, and was grateful for, the efforts

Hemingway did make, and, in a letter of 26 April 1926, thanked Hemingway "for getting me started."

But Hemingway, in fact, did only a few things on behalf of his younger friend. He passed the long story, "Along with Youth," on to Ford Madox Ford at the *transatlantic review* sometime in either late 1924 or early 1925; it was rejected on grounds of length, not quality.[1] By October 1925, Hemingway either showed or promised to show seven stories to the publisher Boni and Liveright; and by April 1926, Hemingway sent "An Autumn Penitent" and "Amuck in the Bush" to Alfred Kreymborg in New York (editor of *The American Caravan* with Van Wyck Brooks, Lewis Mumford, and Paul Rosenfeld). Kreymborg accepted both for publication.

By June 1926 Hemingway had passed all of Callaghan's stories (and his novel) on to Robert McAlmon in Paris who, in turn, showed "Last Spring They Came Over" to *transition*, "A Girl with Ambition" and "A Wedding Dress" to *This Quarter*, and a couple of stories to Ezra Pound who was beginning his magazine, *exile*, in Italy (Letter to Herbst, [1960–61]). McAlmon wrote Callaghan expressing interest in publishing all the material as a book through his Contact Press in Paris, but only if Callaghan could not find another publisher. As Callaghan reported to Hemingway, McAlmon admired the writing, but felt "An Autumn Penitent," with its rural setting and rough-cast characters, was "not quite the thing for Paris and the continent" (Letter to Hemingway, 25 June [1926]).

While Callaghan was sending stories to Hemingway, he was simultaneously mailing stories to publishers on his own behalf. By the autumn of 1925, he had already sent "A Girl with Ambition" to Ernest Walsh at *This Quarter* who asked to see more stories, including "An Autumn Penitent"; by April 1926 he had sent thirteen stories to Edward O'Brien; and by June of the same year he, not Hemingway, had sent "An Autumn Penitent" to Boni and Liveright who rejected it on the grounds that its length, subject matter, and style rendered it "unpublishable" (Letter to Hemingway, 27 Oct. [1926]).

By October, Callaghan sent two more stories to the *New Masses*, the socialist magazine in New York, and some to Marianne Moore's *Dial*. All were rejected. Yet he persisted tenaciously, and by the early spring of 1927, after two years of concerted effort, Callaghan had successfully placed his stories in a variety of magazines. He now entertained plans for publishing a book of stories and the two novels, "An Autumn Penitent" and the still untitled *Strange Fugitive*.

FISSURES IN THE FRIENDSHIP

Callaghan's move away from Hemingway began as early as October 1926. On 22 October, for example, he asked Hemingway, in words that look forward to *That Summer in Paris*,

> Did it ever occur to you how few writers there are who are absolutely open and above board, frank, sincere, and content to say simply what they mean? . . . You practically have to write for yourself, and then you watch the months pass, waiting, God knows what for. Still I'm glad I started here, I think there's a chance of becoming tough, and firm and sort of calmly fierce without getting bitter, and you dont get a chance to talk yourself to death. This is a lot of crap isnt it?

This new, semi-independent tone reappears one month later on 7 November 1926 (in the same letter that praises *The Sun Also Rises*); after complaining that he's written nothing for more than a year, Callaghan baldly states:

> I'll bet a dollar my short stories are good. . . . Better than my novel I guess. The stories being more original would create a slight stir I think. If I get any kind of a break I may yet ask you to write that introduction you once offered to write. I tell you my short stories are good. I can see it now.

The final intellectual, writerly break waited until four months later, on 8 March 1927, when Callaghan wrote to Hemingway expressing his growing sense of discomfort with their friendship:

> the funny thing is that your work had always been some-thing for me to shoot at in the past. . . . Howsomever I feel better about my writing now, and seem to have it more under control, and know what I'm doing which is a delight-ful experience after my many uncertainties. The point is I can't quit now. Often I would have sent you something of mine to read but I've had a feeling that you are busy, or writing a lot yourself. Anyway you seemed to have become rather remote.

Changes had occurred, changes which began to signal an imminent, albeit postponed, rupture in the friendship.

Hemingway, for example, had edited two numbers of the *transatlantic review* while Ford Madox Ford, the regular editor, visited New York in the summer of 1924, a full six months after Hemingway had been in Toronto and had read Callaghan's earliest stories. Hemingway filled the August number with pieces by his friends: John Dos Passos, the inexperienced Nathan Asch, Gertrude Stein, and Guy Hickock — an assemblage that prompted Ford's subsequent wry editorial stating that Heming-way had stuffed the issue with works by his North American friends (Baker, *A Life Story* 129ff).

Why, one wonders, did Hemingway not include any stories by his Canadian friend, Morley Callaghan? If no stories had yet arrived, why didn't he solicit some? If there wasn't enough time, why didn't he use his influence in later issues? It seems decidedly odd that, despite his success with a variety of the Parisian and American magazines, Callaghan published no stories in the *trans-atlantic review* during the twenties and thirties.

This lapse in Hemingway's support leads to yet another ques-tion: why, in the end, was it Robert McAlmon and F. Scott Fitzgerald who were most instrumental in getting Callaghan published for the first time? As Callaghan insisted time and again, it was Fitzgerald who, before ever meeting Callaghan, brought his work to the attention of Max Perkins at Scribner's; it was McAlmon who wrote expressing interest in doing a book of Callaghan's for Contact Press. And indeed, it was McAlmon, not Hemingway, who offered the shrewdest and most penetrating literary criticism in his letters. Why not Hemingway?

It seems the older Hemingway, for all his very real efforts, began to sense the threat of a rival. At first Hemingway had much praise for Callaghan. In a letter to Ernest Walsh on 2 January 1926, in which he praises the issue of *This Quarter* that included both his own "The Undefeated" and Callaghan's "A Girl with Ambition," Hemingway remarks that "of the two I would much rather have written the story by Morley Callaghan" (Baker, *Selected Letters* 187); moreover, on 17 March 1928, Hemingway wrote to Max Perkins at Scribner's that "I was never off of [Callaghan] but only a poor correspondent" (*Selected Letters* 274); and again to Perkins on 11 October 1928, he says he would like to see Callaghan. But by 18 November 1928, in a letter to Fitzgerald, Hemingway sarcastically refers to how "Cops [really] talk" — which is "not as they talk in Callaghan's Works" (*Selected Letters* 290).

Hemingway and Callaghan would experience the crucial crisis of their friendship later in the summer of 1929. Yet it is important to note that, though Hemingway would later insist he had always tried to help Callaghan, in the early summer of 1929 he was already beginning to complain of critical comparisons. On 18 July 1929, for example, he bitterly told Archibald MacLeish that he had been accused of "imitat[ing] Callaghan!" (Baker, *Selected Letters* 300). A year later this irritation ballooned into an accusation of his own: on 12 August 1930 Hemingway snarled to Max Perkins — who was then Callaghan's chief editor — that it was his own "Up in Michigan" that had provided Callaghan with his "source book" (*Selected Letters* 327). The fine young writer who once wrote "big-time stuff" had now, irretrievably, become an enemy. Why?

The true tenor of the friendship seems to lie somewhere

between Hemingway's real respect for Callaghan's writing, his genuinely avuncular interest in helping a younger friend get published, his detestation of himself for actually needing the self-valorization that Callaghan's admiration brought with it, and his own growing discomfort with a disciple gone astray. Perhaps it is this ferocious yet precarious personal ambivalence that accounts for Hemingway's deliberate distancing from the friendship, his deliberate silence in the face of Callaghan's many requests for letters. This may well have been the quality that Callaghan, years later, would describe as Hemingway's "secret need to protect his ego from anyone who might have a minor claim on him" (*That Summer* 233) — the kind of self-protective strategy that was evident in 1923 at the *Star* when Hemingway "seemed to be on the fence about that early Fitzgerald work" (*That Summer* 31).

But the truth seems also to lie somewhere in the changes that were occurring within Callaghan himself. He was now learning, however tentatively, even as he was just starting to write, "the grim lesson that all writers . . . have to learn": "that you can't be sustained by the praise and admiration of a few friends" (*That Summer* 253).[2] The complex nature of these struggles, which began that autumn afternoon in 1923 when Callaghan and Hemingway first met — and which continued submerged in their correspondence from 1925 to 1928 — would become most evident in 1929 during that summer in Paris. For it was then that both men would quarrel over something as simple, as complex, as childish, and as psychologically and culturally loaded, as an amateur boxing match. A contest where Hemingway would fall and Callaghan would dance in dizzying circles, with neither fully realizing that a long simmering fissure in their friendship had finally erupted.

LAW SCHOOL

As influential as Hemingway may have been, he was hardly Callaghan's sole focus of attention in these years. This period, from 1925 to 1928, leading up to his famous trip to Paris, was formative for Callaghan. It was marked by activities and relationships that would provide, if not so direct an influence as Hemingway, then certainly a series of fertile creative experiences in Callaghan's life.

Paramount among these was Callaghan's halfhearted tenure at Osgoode Hall Law School, an undertaking that seems to have been encouraged most strongly by his parents. "If I had to become a lawyer, all right, I would practice law. . . . [T]he obligation to my parents made it necessary for me to finish . . ." (*That Summer* 22, 63). Though these three years of study receive remarkably brief comment in his memoir and interviews, they were hardly insignificant.

On 24 September 1925, while still working part-time at the *Star*, Callaghan began articling with "a plump and amiable young lawyer named Joseph Sedgewick" (*That Summer* 47). Two days later, on 26 September, he entered the law school, Osgoode Hall, simultaneous articling and entrance being normal practice at that time. The received opinion is that Callaghan graduated from Osgoode three years later, was called to the Bar in 1928, then opted for a writing career instead. This version is, to put it simply, inaccurate. Callaghan, in fact, was never a committed student. His studies at Osgoode took a definite back seat to establishing friendships and literary contacts in Paris and New York, to developing his growing relationship with Loretto, and to churning out stories at an astonishingly rapid pace. His entire Osgoode experience was marked by a singularly cavalier, devil-may-care attitude.

In an 11 October 1925 letter to Hemingway, for example, Callaghan comically reports: "I'm now a law student. Have a lot of time and could do a good deal of writing." In his surviving letters to Raymond Knister and such American writers as Nathan Asch, Josephine Herbst, and John Herrmann, he rarely mentions his law studies, only occasionally worrying about an upcoming exam for which he hasn't studied. Likewise, in *That Summer in Paris*, Callaghan unguardedly describes his lukewarm feelings: "I used to go to morning law classes and often doze in my chair. . . . If Joe Sedgewick wanted a title searched I did it for him. Otherwise, with him out on business, I would sit in his office at my typewriter working on a short novel" (47).

The result of such indifference was that Callaghan failed three sets of exams — in June 1927, January 1928, and May 1928 — and was forced to write supplemental examinations in September of 1927 and 1928. He did eventually pass his final year in 1928; thus, according to the regulations of the Law Society at the time, he had every right to be called to the Bar if he so desired. The interesting fact is he didn't. Callaghan freely and consciously decided against it. He rejected a career in law in favour of what had already become his ruling passion.

Notwithstanding his lukewarm attendance, Callaghan's experiences at Osgoode Hall were hardly superficial; they left their mark in more than pragmatic ways. Certainly his training stood him in good stead in later contract negotiations with publishers and in various business ventures over the years. Similarly, he was able to offer free legal advice to friends and fellow writers: sometime in 1928, for example, he advised Raymond Knister about the ins and outs of bond payments, cautioning him at one point to beware double payments (Letter to Knister, [1928]).

But Osgoode seems not so much to have introduced Callaghan to a rich vein of practical resources, as to have consolidated what had been, and would remain, one of his most fertile and challenging areas of literary exploration. Now, in the autumn of 1925, as he explored the dark areas of sexual transgression and public confession in "An Autumn Penitent," Callaghan also pursued what would become a lifelong literary and moral interest in natural justice, transgression, and legality. Law and its mechanisms; the themes of retribution, discipline, penitence, and punishment; an implacable and ultimately unjust justice system — all of these would appear throughout his earliest stories, as well as in his major early novels, *It's Never Over*, *They Shall Inherit the Earth*, and *More Joy in Heaven*. His journalistic columns of the forties, likewise, would return continually to questions of justice, while his major later novels — *The Loved and the Lost, The Many Colored Coat* (with its highly symbolic trial scenes), and *Our Lady of the Snows* — all meticulously employ the vocabulary, philosophies, and technical structures of legal discourse.

Osgoode Hall Law School was only a temporary stop for the rapidly evolving young writer, perhaps merely a token gesture to satisfy his father's aspirations. As a career, law — like the specialized Honours programmes at the University of Toronto — held little attraction for Callaghan's eclectic, enquiring curiosity. But as an intellectual discipline, as a mode of moral, cultural, and ideological analysis, it left its mark across, in, and through the body of Callaghan's work.

Yet this mark was only one of many. The canvas of Callaghan's life now began to crowd with a kaleidoscopic mix of people, activities, and influences. As Callaghan wrote his way through law school, he was beginning to expand his literary and personal operations into the cultural and literary life of Toronto, New York, and, most enticingly, Paris.

THE VIKING LENDING LIBRARY

At the same time that Callaghan was preparing to fail his first set of exams, he launched a gloriously inept business venture with his boyhood friend Art Kent, whose example he had earlier followed in 1923 by joining the staff of the *Star*. By the end of 1926, Callaghan and Art had pooled their savings, rented the basement premises at 69 Richmond Street West in Toronto, and opened the Viking Lending Library, a small bookshop-cum-newsstand from which customers might borrow the most current books for a modest sum. The library was almost immediately a financial fiasco when Art failed to raise his share of the money, but Callaghan struggled on, sinking into debt as he hired one incompetent clerk after another.

As a business, the library was a flop; as a symbolic gesture, a gesture of bohemian culture explicitly mentioned in his interviews and memoir, it was a significant, if not resounding, triumph. Callaghan lovingly described those days to Robert Weaver:

> It lasted two years. . . . I used to sit there at night waiting for Loretta [sic] to join me — and writing stories. I wrote some of my finest stories sitting there at night, and the cop passing slowly on the beat looking down at me. He probably thought I was keeping books, but I was making books. ("Talk" 10)

The Viking was both a writer's hideaway and a curious repetition of Parisian bookshop cafés. In addition to being a library, a study, and a rendezvous, the shop was also — because of Callaghan's interests — the Canadian distributor of such Parisian literary magazines as *This Quarter*. The importance of this role cannot be overestimated, for like Sylvia Beach's famous bookshop Shakespeare and Co. in Paris, the Viking began to evolve into an artists' meeting place, a congenial site of convergence, where writers and artists might gather to create something of a symbolic community. A community within Canada of Canadian outsiders.

Two of Callaghan's most important customers at the Viking were the Canadian writer Raymond Knister, and the American novelist Nathan Asch. Knister, in particular, plays an intriguing role in Callaghan's development as a writer, a role that curiously, almost microcosmically, reenacts and reverses the Hemingway-Callaghan configuration.

RAYMOND KNISTER

One day in either late 1926 or early 1927 Knister — a fellow Canadian who had published poems in the Paris magazines, who had worked on the Chicago magazine, the *Midland*, and who was tuned in to the new literatures of Europe and the United States — introduced himself to Callaghan at the Viking. The two men formed a tenuous, short-lived friendship, with Callaghan, in spite of his relative inexperience and younger age, playing the role he had learned so well from Hemingway: the wiser, more street-smart and publishable mentor.

Callaghan introduced Knister to Greg Clark at the *Star*, for which Knister wrote occasional pieces. Both Knister and Callaghan admired the work coming out of Paris and the United States, and both shared a consciousness of themselves as outsiders in what they perceived to be the Canadian cultural wasteland. As Callaghan remarked to Robert Weaver, "the point is that there were no writers we were in sympathy with. So we were isolated to that extent, but it was fine because we had each other to talk to about writing" ("Talk" 7).

But the discussions and friendship were cut short, partly because of Knister's growing disillusionment. As Callaghan later remarked,

> It seemed to [Knister] that I shot into some kind of a quick success which had been denied him, and I think that sort of embittered him — I mean, not embittered him particularly about me, but it made him feel more isolated, and I think this isolation ate into his soul. ("Talk" 8)

The friendship also suffered because of Callaghan's irritation with what he considered Knister's compromises to popular taste. This irritation would flare up soon in the summer of 1928. In that year Knister edited *Canadian Short Stories* for Macmillan and wrote to Max Perkins at Scribner's, asking and receiving permission to reprint Callaghan's "Last Spring They Came Over." Knister included the story, together with works by such older writers as Duncan Campbell Scott and Gilbert Parker. On 15 August 1928, Callaghan wrote to Knister what must have seemed to the older writer, now living on his farm, an extraordinarily cutting critique:

Dear Raymond,
 Today I got a copy of the Canadian stories. I read the Introduction and then I read D.C. Scott's story in the book. What is the matter with you?

Though it will come as a relief to many schoolmarms throughout the country to learn that the venerable Duncan is a great writer, since they have always suspected it, you know better. Then why do you do it? Are you thinking of retiring definitely? You had a chance to point the way in that introduction, and you merely arrived at the old values that have been accepted here the last fifty years: id est, Duncan C. Scott, G.D. Roberts and Gilbert Parker are great prose writers. In any other country in the world they are not taken seriously. Why do you do it? Since you know better and are willing to put your name to the book. Or is it the mellowing effects of the soil?

The letter reveals a crucial facet of Callaghan's now rapidly developing sense of writerly ideals and integrity. To Callaghan, Knister had sold out to the establishment by including outworn stylists; he could not remain politely silent. Callaghan's unstinting condemnation of Scott, Roberts, and Parker makes explicit his allegiance to the modernist movement, his own furious severance from mainstream Canadian writing. His criticism of Knister, however insensitive and unsentimental it may have been, also reveals what was still (and would remain) an integral part of Callaghan's personality: an uncompromising honesty in the face of what he regarded as deviation from principle. The friendship trickled on for a few more years, with Callaghan writing occasionally thereafter to offer legal advice and literary encouragement, but both men lost contact around 1930, two years before Knister's death in 1932.

NATHAN ASCH

Although Knister and Callaghan shared similar literary ideals, neither felt any particular personal warmth toward the other. As Callaghan remarked in 1958, "Knister was a very rare bird" ("Talk" 8) whose depressions and suspicions sometimes made Callaghan want "to punch him on the nose" (*That Summer* 57).

For a more *simpatico* friend, Callaghan turned to another of his Viking customers, the very different Nathan Asch, whom he had met in New York in 1926.

The New York trip in 1926, in fact, had been a huge success and was soon followed by frequent returns. Not only did Callaghan experience that "first-time-in-New-York-City" buzz, the invigorating sense of finally stepping into the larger, swirling world of the Big Apple, he also finally stepped into the limelight of the literati. By this time Callaghan had begun his correspondence with Robert McAlmon and Hemingway, had stocked the newest New York writers in his small bookshop, and had published "A Girl with Ambition" in *This Quarter*. Hemingway had sent his stories to Alfred Kreymborg in New York; Scribner's was in New York; McAlmon's friends were in New York. The time had come to travel to that other Mecca just south of the border.

In the city and its environs he would dine and drink with established writers: William Carlos Williams, whose poetry he admired; the poet-scholar Allen Tate; the novelist Katherine Ann Porter; and the editor who had sent him his very first rejection letter, Ford Madox Ford. Although Callaghan would continue to correspond with Williams, and would maintain acquaintanceships with the others, during his first visit in 1926 he met three writers in particular with whom he would develop friendships and sustain correspondences for over thirty years: the left-wing proletarian novelist, Josephine Herbst; her husband, John Herrmann; and Nathan Asch, the son of the American novelist, Sholem Asch.

While all four would correspond, visit, and share opinions over the years — especially about the role of the socialist novelist — during the period from 1925 to 1928, Callaghan felt closest to the younger Asch, who would soon become one of his closest American friends. Asch had already visited Paris by this time, and had published in the *transatlantic review* under both Ford's and Hemingway's editorships. He had just published his first novel, *The Office*, in 1925, and offered Callaghan, not simply a connection with New York's community of writers, but more importantly a friendship based on similar interests, ideals, principles, aims, and values.

Their correspondence of this period is filled not only with mutual anxieties about getting published, but with discussions about the merits and demerits of such contemporary writers as Marianne Moore, Sherwood Anderson, Glenway Wescott, and James Tully. Throughout his letters Callaghan consistently develops and corroborates the positions he outlined simultaneously to Hemingway: the new writing must sever its ties with the outworn values and stylizations of a flaccid romanticism; the writer must revolutionize language through crispness, spareness, and imagistic accuracy.

Loretto, who accompanied Callaghan to New York on subsequent trips in 1926 and 1927, liked Nathan Asch, this young man "with his mustache and thick hair and melancholy eyes" (*That Summer* 53); often she sent her regards to Elizabeth, Asch's ailing wife. After 1929, the two couples stayed with each other on convivial visits between Toronto and New York, sharing concerns about spouses, children, and developments in contemporary writing.

Asch circulated some of Callaghan's stories among the New York publishers and was the intermediary between Callaghan and the literary agents Brandt and Brandt who began to act on Callaghan's behalf. Callaghan meanwhile sent frequent letters of advice and support, often sharing his anxiety about the fate of "An Autumn Penitent," which was being held up by Boni and Liveright. When the book was finally rejected by Donald Friede at Boni's, Callaghan wrote to Asch sometime in 1926 or 1927 in an uncharacteristic outpouring: "as for D. Friede. The lousy fucking sonofabitch" (Letter to Asch).

Asch, in fact, became not only a good friend, but a central character in Callaghan's first novel, *Strange Fugitive*, which he began working on at this time. In the summer of 1927, Asch visited Toronto for a month and hung around the Viking. As Callaghan remarked to Robert Weaver years later:

he came up here one summer while I was at Osgoode. He spent most of his time all the time he was in Toronto at that little bookstore. We had an odd little game: we used to play handball at night in the bookstore. You lost a point if the ball didn't hit the edge of the shelf. . . . ("Talk" 9)

Callaghan would thinly disguise Asch, the Viking Library, and himself in *Strange Fugitive*, where Harry Trotter, the gangster hero, and his friend Jimmy Nash, use a bookshop "downtown" as both a front and central office of operations and criminal planning (*Strange Fugitive* 110ff). Like Callaghan and Asch in the Viking, Harry and Nash play handball against the shelves, often spotting a policeman watching them through the windows. The inclusion of such biographical details supplements Callaghan's overall gangsterization of himself throughout the book, an intriguing displacement of his own self-consciously subversive writing activities.

★   ★   ★

What Callaghan tried to — and did — create in his small bookshop was a Canadian equivalent of the European cultural café, a symbolic meeting place for contemporary artists like Knister and Asch, a place which, in its self-conscious connections with Paris, lent an air of respectable bohemianism to the staid Toronto that surrounded it. Given its crucial symbolic, social, and psychic significance for Callaghan, the fact that it was a commercial failure after two years is, ultimately, irrelevant. What counted was the fact that the Viking became one more vehicle through which he moved forward in his chosen world of contemporary writing. Less a commercial venture than a symbolic place, the Viking constituted for Callaghan "a room of his own" in the Canadian house of his literary forebears.

By the end of 1927, as Callaghan steadily pursued his overlapping interests and responsibilities — Osgoode, the Viking Library, literary friendships, and creative writing — things swiftly began to fall into place. He had only one year of law school remaining; he had begun to form crucial connections with other writers; Loretto and he were cementing their relationship. Four stories had been published in Paris and New York; "An Autumn Penitent" would soon appear in *The Second American Caravan*; "A Country Passion" had been accepted by Eugene Jolas for *transition*; and Ezra Pound wrote from Italy that he would publish both "A Predicament" and "Ancient Lineage" in his magazine, *exile*. Callaghan and Loretto decided to celebrate: they bought a chicken and some wine, and wrote to Nathan Asch who, in turn, cabled his congratulations over the Pound acceptance.

In January of 1928, Callaghan travelled to New York once again. The trip was pressing and anxiety-provoking because he had by this time completed *Strange Fugitive* (then called "Big Boy"), and it was now in the hands of Scribner's in New York. Its editor, Max Perkins, had initially rejected the manuscript with considerable reluctance, but had written via Brandt asking to see more stories and expressing interest in publishing "A Predicament" if Pound would release it. Callaghan later sent Perkins an expanded version of the novel — yet Perkins still had not mentioned it. The time had come for Callaghan to return to New York.

"Wondering how everything had happened so swiftly, wondering, too, if Hemingway had spoken to Perkins" (*That Summer* 57), Callaghan set out by train in the cold early months of 1928 to meet with Perkins, to find out what fate — and Scribner's — had in store for him. What Callaghan discovered was astonishing.

He learned from Max Perkins himself that he had been brought to the attention of Scribner's by none other than F. Scott Fitzgerald, not Hemingway, whom Perkins didn't realize was a friend of Callaghan's. (Though apparently Brandt had also been passing along stories to Scribner's.) Perkins had admired

Callaghan's "Amuck in the Bush," which appeared in *The American Caravan*, and mentioning this to Fitzgerald, learned of Callaghan's other stories in the Paris magazines. His appetite whetted, Perkins wrote to Callaghan in 1926, who sent both a story and the manuscript of *Strange Fugitive*. Amazed and confused at what seemed a cavalier indifference on the part of Hemingway, and pleased by the unexpected enthusiasm of Fitzgerald whom he had never met, Callaghan now learned in Cheerio's restaurant that Scribner's had plans for him. Big plans.

As the voluminous Scribner's correspondence reveals, Perkins initially wanted to publish a collection of Callaghan's short stories because he felt that "Big Boy" (*Strange Fugitive*) wasn't quite ready for publication. He had been especially impressed with Callaghan's "A Predicament," which Pound had released to Scribner's, at Callaghan's own request, in late 1926 or early 1927 (Letter to Pound, [1926]). After Callaghan added about 20,000 words to "Big Boy," Perkins changed his plans and agreed to publish the novel first — now entitled *Strange Fugitive* — to be followed the next year by a collection of stories. His prospects changed forever, Callaghan returned to Toronto filled with elation at his sudden triumph. But he also harboured a multitude of insecurities: what had happened with Hemingway?

The remainder of 1928 and beginnings of 1929 were occupied with preparations on all fronts. His law studies had to be completed; exams were now looming on the spring horizon. Wedding plans were afoot, with the date set for 16 April 1929, the week before Callaghan and Loretto would depart for Paris! Callaghan was also writing at a feverish pitch.

In spite of Hemingway's earlier advice to the contrary — that reviews were a waste of time and creative energy — Callaghan began what would amount to nine monthly literary reviews for *Saturday Night*, beginning on 12 May 1928. Here he not only championed Ford Madox Ford, William Carlos Williams, and Virginia Woolf, but he also introduced Toronto readers to European innovators such as Liam O'Flaherty, Thomas Mann, and Henri Barbusse. In his critiques and evaluations, he continued to hone his aesthetic credo: "Tell the truth cleanly" (*That Summer* 20).

Amidst this flurry of enthusiasm, a trifling occurrence set into motion something that both Callaghan and Hemingway would resent and ultimately deride for the rest of their lives. In April 1928, Scribner's publicity department wrote to Callaghan, asking if he objected to their plans to link him with Hemingway in their advertisements. Callaghan's reply was hesitant, for he resisted being placed on the Hemingway bandwagon. Scribner's replied in May 1928, agreeing with Callaghan, but by July they had recanted and went ahead with the infamous advertisement, publishing two of Callaghan's stories in the July 1928 issue of *Scribner's Magazine*, thereby linking him with Hemingway: "It will be remembered that on the other occasion when we presented two stories in the same number the writer was Ernest Hemingway" (qtd. in Conron, *Morley Callaghan* [1966] 34–35).

Once again Callaghan was drawn reluctantly into Hemingway's orbit. Scribner's decision would ultimately cause more harm than good: both Callaghan and Hemingway would begin to resent the comparisons, and subsequent critics would predictably place Callaghan in the shadow of the older American. Following the lead of Scribner's advertisement in July 1928 — that Callaghan was a younger disciple of Hemingway — critics, such as Fraser Sutherland in *The Style of Innocence*, consistently placed Callaghan in the apprentice role. This biased reading of the Hemingway-Callaghan relationship continually addressed the vexed issue of literary influence which, at the time, plagued the friendship of the two men. Arguing for Callaghan's essential belatedness, the "pro-Hemingway" school views Callaghan's early activity as a schoolboy imitation of Hemingway's techniques, themes, and subject matter. Certainly the younger writer did experiment with Hemingway's methods, but these methods were themselves experiments with the writings of Anderson, Suckow, Dreiser, Conrad, and Hardy. The point is that Callaghan and Hemingway were both young writers; both were engaged in an intertextual struggle with their contemporaries; and both were apprentices in the craft of fiction. But each would take different paths; each would evolve a distinctive method borne out of his own — not the other's — struggles with verbal form. As Callaghan complained in later years, "You have to have some kind of a view of life. My view of life was not Fitzgerald's view of life, and certainly anybody capable of passing an entrance exam ought to have seen years ago that it's not Hemingway's view of life" ("Talk" 25).

Yet as 1928 drew to a close, Callaghan was well on his way to personal and literary success. He was finished with Osgoode, fulfilling his obligations to his parents, and providing himself with a workable trade if all else failed. He had journalistic experience up his sleeve and, though the bookshop had long fizzled, he had used it well as a stepping ground between New York and Paris. By the spring of the following year, he would be married to the woman he loved, and he'd be known in literary circles on both sides of the Atlantic. In one sense he felt the world was opening up to him: he was young, robust, smart — and he was published. He was friends with such writers as Josephine Herbst, John Herrmann, Nathan Asch, and Ernest Hemingway; he had met William Carlos Williams, Ford Madox Ford, Katherine Ann Porter, and Allen Tate. He was also on joking terms with the editors of Scribner's and enjoyed a voluminous and personable correspondence with Max Perkins.

All that was left to make things perfect was to visit the city of his dreams. Springtime in Paris — he had no doubt it would be magnificent. Accordingly, Callaghan finished the year in a swirl of writing, love, and optimism. Dreaming about the city of light, he was little aware that he would soon tread within a nightmarish circle of disillusioned friends, vicious recriminations, and lost innocence.

THE VOYAGE OUT

April 1929 saw both Callaghan and Loretto in high spirits. They married on 16 April in Toronto and set out the following week on a six-month honeymoon, a European journey of discovery

FIGURE 4

Loretto Callaghan in 1929.

that neither would ever forget. They travelled first to New York where Max Perkins organized a meeting with one of Callaghan's favourite American writers, Sinclair Lewis. The meeting both impressed and depressed Callaghan. Although his opinion of Lewis as a great writer was accentuated by Lewis's personal warmth, Callaghan realized that Lewis's peculiar ability to entice a reader also constituted one of his great weaknesses: the reader was always too comfortable, too unchallenged by a style that remained always too familiar.

After a few days in New York the Callaghans embarked by boat for France, where they stayed initially in the same Paris hotel as Robert McAlmon — the Paris-New York Hotel on Rue Vaugirard. Then, with the help of John Glassco, a fellow Canadian from Montreal who would later pillory Callaghan as a gauche bumpkin in his *Memoirs of Montparnasse*, they found a small apartment over a grocery shop at 15 Rue de la Santé. Here, overlooking the local prison, Callaghan was exultant, finally able to see with his own eyes the city of Baudelaire, Zola, and Balzac.

For Callaghan, Paris wasn't simply an exotic city, merely providing him an opportunity to gain overseas experience. It was, rather, a symbol of his own desire — a city that encapsulated the values and excitements of his soul. As he remarks in *That Summer in Paris*:

It offered the climate, the ambience, the importance of the recognition of the new for the artist. In those days a writer coming to Paris could believe he would find contemporaries. . . . [T]he Paris of those days had become like a giant crystal; like a crystal with many facets, and the French had a genius for turning and ever turning the crystal so the light would fall on a new facet, and then from the cafés would come the announcement, "This is the way it is being looked at now." (114–15)

Paris had become the centre of innovation, a site of convergence where the newest and most experimental artists gathered, competed, created, and were created. It was the centre of expatriate writing: Hemingway, Joyce, and Fitzgerald were based here; it was the locale of the most avant-garde literary magazines and publishers — *This Quarter, transition, transatlantic review*, McAlmon's Contact Press, Edward Titus's Black Mannikin bookshop. All represented for Callaghan the crystallization of what he had set out to do as early as 1923: to articulate a new vision, a new form of handling the language distinct from the established idiom. Finally he had arrived: he was a *real* writer living amongst writers.

THAT SUMMER IN PARIS

Callaghan continued to write at a rapid pace and by August 1929 had completed his second novel, *It's Never Over*, for Scribner's. That month, when he sent the manuscript to Max Perkins, he was troubled, as usual, about an appropriate title, and wanted either "It's Never Over," "The Possessed," "Dark Interval," or "Treading the Shadows" (Letter to Perkins, [1929]). Both Scribner's and the *New Yorker* solicited more stories, and Callaghan worked on "The Faithful Wife" and "The Chiseller." He also wrote "Now That April's Here" — a story about a homosexual couple — at the suggestion of Edward Titus, and began work on the sexually risqué novella, *No Man's Meat*, which Titus, who had published D.H. Lawrence's *Lady Chatterley's Lover*, would print in 1931 through his prestigious Black Mannikin Press. During this summer Callaghan also began to tease out plans for a third novel, *A Broken Journey*, which Scribner's would later publish in 1932.

It is astonishing, given this output, that Callaghan found time for anything other than writing. But he and Loretto were blessed with a growing lust for living in the here and now. Paris was alive with expatriates in the summer of 1929, young men and women floating blithely through the halcyon days before the depression, blissfully unaware of the impending stock market crash of October 1929. The Callaghans' days were leisure-filled, their mood a mix of exultant curiosity and intense intellectual excitement. During May and June they "did" the café circuit, sipping pernod, seeing and being seen, playfully arguing with the local celebrities: Ludwig Lewisohn, Michael Arlen, Kay Boyle, Ford Madox Ford, and Allen Tate.

The intellectual circles were dominated by the rise of fascists and the hopes of Marxist revolutionaries. The Callaghans also met local painters — notably Joan Miró — and entered fully into the swirl of literary and artistic life. They visited painters' lofts, partied till dawn, attended readings, and once even wandered into a brothel by mistake — a bohemian life which Callaghan would recall almost sixty years later in *A Wild Old Man on the Road*.

Much of the time the Callaghans socialized with Robert McAlmon who had first helped Callaghan get published and who now introduced them to writers and artists in the quarter. Though McAlmon could be a bitter and difficult companion, one who continually criticized and scandalized his friends and enemies through his gossip and bisexual antics, he and the Callaghans remained on friendly terms. For Callaghan, McAlmon was simply a gifted artist who lacked discipline, a complex man of quiveringly intense sensibilities unbound by convention. Through McAlmon the Callaghans met James and Nora Joyce, with whom they enjoyed a tipsy evening, killing a bottle of scotch, telling jokes, and giggling over unintentionally ribald *double entendres* — "Come, come on to me" — in a recording by the American evangelist, Aimee Semple McPherson (*That Summer* 138–45).

After a hot July during which they housesat for Edward Titus, the Callaghans travelled south through Bayonne, Biarritz, Lourdes, and Pamplona, where, like Hemingway, they watched the famous run of bulls. The next few weeks flickered by as, one by one, the artists of the quarter began to leave, Hemingway to Spain, Fitzgerald to Nice. By early September the Callaghans returned to Paris and began to pack up, leaving midmonth for London and Dublin where they stayed for two weeks.

By mid-October the summer in Paris had ended, and the Callaghans returned to Toronto. After staying for a month or so with first Morley's and then Loretto's parents, Callaghan and Loretto set up their first apartment in Toronto where Callaghan now resumed work on *A Broken Journey*.

SPARRING WITH HEMINGWAY

If Paris for Callaghan functioned primarily as a symbol of desire, it was also a fulcrum of personal and professional change where he would revive one of his most significant early friendships. The city had offered, above all else, the chance to renew his friendship with an old mentor: in April 1929, he was delighted at the prospect of meeting up again with Hemingway, wondering quietly if it would be possible to clear up the growing doubts and simmering insecurities that had surfaced between them.

At first it seemed that a happy outcome was imminent. Hemingway responded promptly to Callaghan's letter announcing their arrival in Paris. Visiting the Paris-New York Hotel unannounced, he immediately took Callaghan and Loretto to meet his second wife, Pauline, and their young baby son. Learning now for the first time that Callaghan had boxed at university, Hemingway was delighted to have a workout partner at his gym, The American Club. Both men spent the next few weeks boxing, enjoying the male ritual of a good workout followed by drinks and conversation. Though not as fit as he would have liked, Callaghan could box well enough, and initially Hemingway enjoyed the challenge. He wrote to Max Perkins on 24 June 1929: "I have seen Morley Callaghan several times and boxed with him five times I think. He has not the appearance but is an *excellent* boxer" (Baker, *Selected Letters* 299).

However, this boxing camaraderie did not last long. Sometime in early July it soured suddenly, coincident with the arrival of F. Scott Fitzgerald who had also become friendly with the Callaghans. It was Fitzgerald, in fact, who first read and constructively criticized Callaghan's draft of *It's Never Over*. All three writers would have an irretrievable falling-out centred, ostensibly, on something as apparently minor as a sparring match in a half-deserted gymnasium.

What happened in July of 1929 seems now almost pathetic, if not bathetic. The facts are simple enough: one day in early July Fitzgerald acted as timekeeper as Callaghan and Hemingway worked out. Fitzgerald let one round go longer than the agreed upon time; Callaghan punched Hemingway in the mouth and Hemingway fell to the floor. Realizing that the round had gone overtime, Hemingway became angry and accused Fitzgerald of deliberately allowing the clock to run over. In his own eyes, he felt humiliated. But apologies were quickly proffered all around, the three men laughed it off, and afterwards they went out for drinks. By late August the incident seemed to have been forgotten: Hemingway socialized with Callaghan and Loretto and, on their last day in France, took them on a whirlwind tour of Chartres.

But the consequences of that July bout were anything but simple. Hemingway had begun to enjoy a reputation of being macho, a public image based on such masculinist values as strength, courage, and physical savagery. News of the boxing match soon circulated in exaggerated rumours throughout the Montparnasse circuit: Hemingway, the great bear of the American expatriates, apparently had been knocked cold by the young, pudgy Canadian. After Callaghan and Loretto returned to Toronto in October, the rumour ballooned and quickly reached New York, where, in late November, Isabel Patterson ran a gossipy story in the *Herald Tribune* that showed Hemingway in a ridiculous light: Hemingway appeared a braggart and a fool, a hack who had been severely and rightly thumped by Callaghan.

Initially Hemingway was furious. Boxing had hardly been an idle pastime; as Callaghan's fighting metaphors throughout *That Summer in Paris* suggest, the sport functioned as a highly charged metaphor of Hemingway's artistic and personal self-worth. Good boxing was a physical analogue of good artistry. Rumours of being knocked out were emotionally, psychically, and artistically unbearable. Believing that Callaghan himself had circulated the story, Hemingway, who was now back in Paris, insisted that Fitzgerald cable Callaghan to demand an apology. In early December Fitzgerald did indeed send the cable, saying that both he and Hemingway awaited Callaghan's public correction of the story.

Although Callaghan did not share this particular macho investment in the boxing match, he was hardly disinterested. As an amateur athlete and a man of the 1920s, when physical prowess and strength were socially endorsed masculine qualities, he hardly wished to appear a weakling. Furthermore, as a young man who placed considerable importance on loyalty and friendship, and as a young writer grateful to his friend for his help, he had an understandable investment in not appearing a cheap rumour-monger.

The surviving letters between Max Perkins and Callaghan, and between Callaghan and Josephine Herbst, clearly show that while Hemingway was fuming in Paris, Callaghan not only wrote letters to both Isabel Patterson and Max Perkins clarifying what had really happened, but he also maintained an ordinary correspondence with Herbst, blithely talking about family matters, Toronto, and the difficulties of finding a new apartment. Callaghan obviously realized that Hemingway was upset, but he saw the event for what it was: a piddling bit of literary gossip that needed to be corrected.

However, events continued to snowball. After Patterson printed Callaghan's explanation in early December — that he and Hemingway had simply worked out together and that there had been no spectacular knockout — Callaghan wrote an angry letter to Fitzgerald, expressing his exasperation at his and Hemingway's overreaction. By this time Hemingway had also written angry letters to Fitzgerald (on 12 December 1929) and Perkins (on 15 December 1929) expressing his intense disillusionment with Callaghan. Finally on 4 January 1930, after reading Callaghan's public letter to Patterson, Hemingway wrote to

Callaghan himself, acknowledging his error in attributing the story to him. Hemingway admitted that it was probably one of his many literary enemies, Pierre Loving — though Carlos Baker suggests the Denver journalist Caroline Bancroft (206) — who had circulated the story in New York, and that it was he, Hemingway, who had pressured Fitzgerald to cable Callaghan. But the letter ends on a sour note: "If you wish to transfer to me the epithets you applied to Scott I will be in the States in a few weeks and am at your disposal any place where there is no publicity attached" (Baker, *Selected Letters* 319).

That famous fight in Paris was, one could say, the straw that broke both camels' backs. Hemingway's subsequent letters to Perkins, Guy Hickock, Ivan Kashkin, and Arthur Mizener reveal his intense antagonism towards Callaghan, whom he now felt was not only a lousy boxer, but an opportunistic amateur who had betrayed his trust, help, and genuine interest. Although Hemingway occasionally insisted that he had nothing against Callaghan as a writer, and although he eventually wrote in a conciliatory fashion about Callaghan to Max Perkins and others, his letters continued to be derogatory. Overall, they attest to the emotional intensity with which Hemingway finally withdrew from the friendship.

Callaghan, on the other hand, retained a dignified and pained public silence on the matter, waiting until 1963 to publish his own version of events in *That Summer in Paris* — a version consistently corroborated by the Scribner's correspondence. Callaghan would, in later years, occasionally hear of Hemingway from mutual friends; and, toward the end of his life, Hemingway would ask after Callaghan, wondering what had happened to his Canadian friend. Eventually the fierce emotions of the late twenties were clouded by time.

But at the beginning of 1930, Callaghan solidly embarked on his writing career without his American friend, without what had been one of his crucial, sustaining early friendships. The fight, in all its rich metaphoric possibility, terminated once and for all this first major literary connection. It also marked the end of the first phase of Callaghan's writing career; the thirties would witness major changes in his life, in his thought, and above all else, in his artistic development.

ABSOLUTIONS

The decade opened immediately after a near fatal car crash in late December 1929. Callaghan and Loretto, returning to Toronto from New York, swerved to avoid a truck on an icy road. They ended in a ditch, bruised and shaken, but the accident was, thankfully, no ill omen. The thirties proved to be one of Callaghan's most prolific — and restless — periods. His two sons were born in this decade: Michael in November 1931 and Barry in July 1937. The family shifted residences nine times over the next ten years, affecting Callaghan's writing, which acquired a strongly nomadic texture, one of continually shifting intellectual directions.

Even the most cursory glance over Callaghan's bibliography for this period reveals an incredible output: he published six novels, sixty-five short stories (thirty-five of which were collected in *Now That April's Here*), thirteen journalistic articles, and twenty-eight literary reviews. A lifetime's work for some — in seven years!

Much more significant are the intellectual shifts identifiable in Callaghan's aesthetic output in these years. On one hand, novels like *It's Never Over*, *No Man's Meat*, and *A Broken Journey* continued to display the profound influences of American naturalists such as Sherwood Anderson and Theodore Dreiser; on the other, the great religious triad of *Such Is My Beloved*, *They Shall Inherit the Earth*, and *More Joy in Heaven* marked the emergence of a distinctive and more theologically inquiring voice. Though Callaghan would always be a somewhat heretical Roman Catholic, he now pursued a peculiarly committed form of Christian philosophy, developed in large part from his personal friendship with the French neo-Thomist philosopher, Jacques Maritain. Although

Callaghan did occasionally attend mass, he rarely followed orthodox Catholic rituals. His was an individualistic, highly personal form of Catholicism.

The stories, though they continued to achieve a transparent colloquialism, also moved toward a more subtly spiritual, less deterministic, exploration of personal morality. Callaghan's reviews and articles, while continuing to emphasize his interest in European and American writing, began to address questions of Canadian nationalism, local boosterism, and the idea of a "native" Canadian prose. Morley Callaghan, the American naturalist, was beginning to see Canada — and God — through his own post-Parisian eyes.

Although Callaghan left Paris in the autumn of 1929, Paris never really left Callaghan. Its ever-turning, multidimensional crystal coloured his writing well after his return to Toronto. In one sense, Paris provided Callaghan with an explosive, almost carnivalesque affirmation of what was his own already established antiauthoritarian perspective. In Paris and its environs he had not only hobnobbed with artists, visited cafés, and written novels, but he and Loretto had also experienced the alternative European worlds of the decadent, the surreal, and the transgressive. Imagine the Toronto boy once forbidden by city bureaucrats to toboggan on Sundays now staring wide-eyed with his new wife as they mistakenly wandered into a Biarritz brothel! There they were, blithely offered by the madam their choice of the brothel's peculiar brand of tableau: staged scenes in which the prostitutes posed in various frozen moments of sexual activity (*That Summer* 225).

Europe in general, and Paris in particular, exposed Callaghan to this other order — an alternative life to the rigid puritanism of Toronto. This carnal absolution took firm hold: for though Callaghan would rarely detail explicit lovemaking in his novels, they now invariably contained unmistakable undercurrents of jaded sexuality and contorted desire. From here on, the novels would be filled with prostitutes, criminals, and petty thieves.

But Callaghan's experience of Paris was double-edged: the

vision of this urban underworld also took away some of his easy confidences, replacing them with a more sophisticated and demanding philosophical life code. His early beliefs and convictions about Christianity, about innocence, even about writing and morality, underwent profound change. Callaghan never embraced Henry Miller's existential hedonism or Hemingway's masculinist code of behaviour. On the contrary, what Callaghan did draw on was one crucial filament of Parisian intellectual life: the alternative world of sceptical religious spirituality.

Though this spiritual dimension seemed conspicuously absent in the summer of 1929, theological and philosophical speculation was ever-present in Callaghan's reading and thinking, especially in Paris. As he remarked to Hemingway in an early letter, "as for Mother Church, I have a real amateur interest in theological questions and some skill in disputation after the fashion of the Schoolmen" (Letter to Hemingway, 12 Aug. [1926]). After Paris, this skill would be finely honed: Callaghan would explore a peculiarly heretical spirituality, a quasi-Catholic philosophy, throughout the novels of his next major creative phase.

A BROKEN JOURNEY

After their return to Toronto in October 1929, the Callaghans stayed briefly with Callaghan's parents at 35 Woolfrey Avenue before signing a six-month lease in early November at 516 Riverside Drive. As early as February 1930, however, Callaghan was again struck with wanderlust and felt the seductive allure of New York. In March he wrote to his friend Josephine Herbst — with whom he would correspond until her death in 1969 — complaining that he and Loretto had tired of Toronto, and asked if she and her husband, John Herrmann, could let them their farmhouse in Pennsylvania (Letter to Herbst, 20 Mar. [1930]). From May until the end of December 1930, the Callaghans alternated residences between the Herbst-Herrmann farmhouse in Pennsylvania and the Madison Hotel in New York City.

Times were extraordinarily tough for everyone: the depression gained firm hold of the economy; unemployment was rampant. The publishing industry, especially, entered hard times; indeed, the letters of Callaghan, Herbst, and Max Perkins continually emphasize financial problems. It is remarkable that during this economically depressed period Callaghan supported Loretto and himself solely by publishing novels, stories, and literary reviews.

It's Never Over came out on 28 February 1930; plans were well under way for Edward Titus to publish *No Man's Meat* in Paris; and *Strange Fugitive* had been reprinted by Scribner's. Through the good graces of Max Perkins, Scribner's advanced Callaghan the princely sum of $150 on the reprint. While living between Pennsylvania and New York, Callaghan sold stories at a furious pace, not only to Scribner's, but also to the *Canadian Magazine* and the *New Yorker*, earning enough to live modestly but well. The *Star* had taken a few pieces in late 1929, and as the thirties advanced, Callaghan became a regular reviewer for *Saturday Night*.

But what dominated his time in the last eight months of 1930, the entirety of 1931, and the first part of 1932 (as he moved often around Toronto) was not the stories; it was the new novel, tentatively titled "Not without Honor." Continuing the risqué direction of *No Man's Meat*, Callaghan embarked on the unconventional story of Marion Gibbons and her mother, both of whom are locked in sexual rivalry over the same man, Peter Gould. If the plot seemed demanding, the execution of it was almost intolerable. As the decade proceeded, with the Callaghans camping in Northern Ontario in the summers of 1931 and 1932, Callaghan was taking forever with the revisions. He constantly sent Max Perkins instructions and alterations, in each case excising melodramatic overstatements and all-too-explicit sexual descriptions.

By October 1931, Callaghan was furious with Perkins's call for major revisions, countering with his own conviction that this novel was already "much more interpretive than my other books" (Letter to Perkins, 20 Oct. [1931]). But Perkins's opinion prevailed, and by February of the next year Callaghan buckled down and completed the revisions. By June 1932, the manuscript having appeared in proofs, Callaghan wrote with yet more minor alterations and one request: he wanted to dedicate the book, now called *A Broken Journey*, to "Loretto and Michael" — for "good luck" (Letter to Perkins, 14 June [1932]).

In one sense *A Broken Journey* uses the conventional love triangle to follow the well-worn Dreiserian path of American naturalism. By focusing on the psychological processes of mother, daughter, and lover — indeed focusing voyeuristically on their transgressive desires — Callaghan examined (sometimes awkwardly) the determining effects of history and biology. In addition, the novel reveals his often overlooked fondness for literary parody: Marion's brief affair with a rural woodsman subtly deflates the more extravagant earthiness of D.H. Lawrence's Mellors in *Lady Chatterley's Lover*.

But Callaghan's large, ungainly book marked the beginnings of a major turning point. Throughout this transgressive drama Callaghan presents a parable of spiritual odyssey in the hopeless Catholicism of Mrs. Gibbons. Interestingly, he also continued what had by now become the habit of recycling earlier stories: chapters two and twelve of the novel are both revised versions of earlier short stories about young priests.[3]

If *A Broken Journey* continued the directions initiated in *Strange Fugitive* and *It's Never Over* (and to some extent *No Man's Meat*), it also, however embryonically, expressed Callaghan's growing interest in spirituality. As Callaghan remarked to Perkins on 29 May 1932,

It is true that the first theme is the love of Peter and Marion; but the secondary theme, the journey, should be a symbol for all their youthful aspirations, in fact a symbol above the story, of a kind of spiritual goal. The reader should feel that this journey becomes for the characters a theological necessity, if such a term explains it. (Letter to Perkins)

After nearly two years of work the book finally appeared in September 1932. Callaghan was exultant: he felt it was the best thing he had written to date. But not everyone agreed; the book, unsurprisingly, received mixed reviews. Though Callaghan was praised for his "fine, vivid prose full of concrete images," he was also panned for his obscurity, "fumbling passages," and heavy "monotony" (Daniels 40, 41). Sadly, such critiques continually overlooked his linguistic experimentation and complex ideas. Instead they returned again and again to the tired comparisons with Hemingway, Anderson, Dreiser — and now even Maupassant! Such comparisons were ironic, for it was precisely at this point in his writing career — both in verbal style and novelistic form — that Callaghan had abandoned his American mentors and begun to strike out in new directions. He was pushing to the limit the capabilities of his own peculiar literary language, not to mention the limits of his Roman Catholicism, which, soon after the publication of *A Broken Journey*, underwent profound alterations thanks to the French neo-Thomist philosopher, Jacques Maritain.

JACQUES MARITAIN'S
THEOCENTRIC HUMANISM

A leading light in the French Catholic revival, Maritain had begun, in the winter of 1933, the first of a series of visits as occasional professor at the University of Toronto's Pontifical Institute of Medieval Studies. He was largely responsible for the vogue during the twenties of renewed Christian personalism, a theocentric humanism which French intellectuals were using to counter the cancerous growth of European fascism. As Callaghan would later remark in a letter to Josephine Herbst, "[Maritain] is trying hard to combat the wave of Fascism which is really rolling over France now, and he will be as instrumental in defeating it among the young, if it is to be defeated, as anyone will be" (Letter to Herbst, 10 Feb. 1936).

In Maritain, especially in his *Art and Scholasticism* which first appeared in 1920, Callaghan found a singularly kindred spirit. Like Callaghan, Maritain was a religious thinker who believed that a "single human soul is of more worth than the whole universe of bodies and material goods. There is nothing above the human soul except God" (*Rights of Man* 13). Yet also like Callaghan, he was keenly aware that human beings live within the material world. As such, he would argue in *True Humanism* that the authentic saint never disallows the importance of materiality: the saint loves men and women as they are "loved by God, and made by Him as fair and worthy of our love. For to love beings in and for God is not to treat them as a mere means or a mere occasion for loving God, but to love and cherish their being as an end, because it *merits* love . . ." (65).[4]

Callaghan had read Maritain during his undergraduate days at the University of Toronto and in *That Summer in Paris* remarks that "Christian artists were finding new dignity and spiritual adventure in [his] neo-Thomism . . ." (94). But now, in 1933, Callaghan finally met Maritain through his close friend Manny Chapman, a Jewish convert who taught philosophy in Chicago and was himself visiting the Pontifical Institute in Toronto.

The relationship between Maritain, Chapman, Callaghan, and Loretto was warm and congenial. Maritain took a genuine liking to Callaghan and Loretto. He and Chapman often dined at the Callaghans' new apartment at 46 Avenue Road, usually staying until the early hours, rapt in conversation and good-natured debate. Their topics ranged the full gamut one might expect of such a motley crew: from Aquinas to prostitution, from art and morality to the nature of sainthood.

SUCH IS MY BELOVED

One evening these conversations took a particular turn which would result three months later in one of Canada's best known novels: *Such Is My Beloved*, the story of Father Stephen Dowling, a young priest who befriends two prostitutes in Toronto. The source of Callaghan's story has always been a vexed question for Canadian critics. Some have suggested he stumbled upon the plot in a newspaper article; others, less charitably inclined, have hinted the story is vaguely autobiographical and that Callaghan's "M" in the dedication is actually Midge, the real-life counterpart to one of the story's prostitutes. The facts are much more intriguing.

From a letter written by Callaghan to Max Perkins on 3 September 1933, we know the true nature of the novel's conception and development. One evening at Avenue Road, when the conversation turned to the problem of prostitution, Maritain told the sad story of a young priest he knew back in Paris. The young man had befriended two prostitutes, tried to help them materially, but when the news broke and scandal erupted, the experience shattered his spirit. The priest had had a nervous breakdown and was now cloistered in a French monastery, deranged and broken-spirited. Maritain was personally saddened by these events, particularly since he'd known the young priest quite well.

At this point Callaghan was in the middle of a new novel, possibly an early draft of *They Shall Inherit the Earth*, which was published a mere twelve months after *Such Is My Beloved*. He had, in fact, already written over 30,000 words. But Maritain's anecdote affected him so powerfully that he abandoned this work-in-progress and, in a "grand passion," wrote *Such Is My Beloved* between late February or early March and May 1933 (Letter to Perkins, 14 June [1933]).

At first he was filled with a mixture of exultation and trepidation: the story's possibilities mesmerized him, but he was unwilling to betray what he felt Maritain might consider a confidential anecdote. After a number of consultations, however, and prompted by Manny Chapman, Maritain himself encouraged Callaghan to write the story. Maritain felt that if it gained a wide readership it would not only publicly celebrate a humanistic Catholicism, but it might also, conceivably, vindicate the actions of his young friend (Letter to Perkins, 3 Sept. [1933]).

By early June, Callaghan finished the final typescript and confidently sent copies to Ann Watkins, his New York agent, and Max Perkins. But with the greatest of trepidation he waited until September to send a copy to Maritain, who by then had returned to France. Callaghan worried that *Such Is My Beloved* would not meet Maritain's expectations. Another complication was that he wished to dedicate the book to Maritain, but Scribner's wanted to quote the philosopher in its advertising blurbs. This not only would have made Callaghan appear sycophantic, but it might also have appeared to link Maritain with the book's subject matter, possibly placing him in some jeopardy within conservative Catholic circles. Callaghan finally compromised, agreeing to dedicate the book, "To Those Times with M. in the Winter of 1933." He also agreed to ask Maritain himself, writing in mid-September, for permission for Scribner's to quote from one of his letters in their advertising blurb.

By mid-December Maritain finally answered, offering both praise and criticism. Callaghan related Maritain's comments to Perkins in December 1933. Critically speaking, Maritain felt the book lacked "poetic profundity": its characters imposed themselves too much from the outside rather than the inside, lacking psychological and emotional depth. Father Dowling's madness seemed to develop far too abruptly; and the women's language bordered too often on the shocking. On the positive side, Maritain emphasized that he had no theological objections. He believed Callaghan had two crucial talents of the artist: "the gift of emotion and pity in the heart and the gift of simplicity in art" (Letter to Perkins, 18 Dec. [1933]). Most importantly, Maritain also gave permission to use his comments on the book's jacket: "I have been profoundly touched by the absolute sincerity of this very moving book" (Letter to Perkins, 18 Dec. [1933]). After three nervous months, Callaghan was jubilant.

His negotiations with Scribner's and Maritain finally at an end, the problems of the dedication and advertising material equitably solved, Callaghan settled down, a touch ruefully, to enjoy the Christmas holidays in Toronto. Ruefully because by now, after four years back in dull puritan Toronto, he had high hopes that *Such Is My Beloved* would "do well enough to set me free of Toronto and Canada for a while, for the place gets greyer and greyer for me. My forty days in the desert may become days without end" (Letter to Perkins, 11 Jan. [1934]).

But the novel, like virtually all of Callaghan's books for Scribner's, sold poorly, a disappointment for both publisher and author. However, *Such Is My Beloved* did remarkably well in terms of Callaghan's international critical reputation and his own spiritual morale. In the April edition of the *Forum and Century*, Mary M. Colum praised Callaghan's "depth of emotion and . . . range of sympathy" (48), qualities she felt he had in abundance over both F. Scott Fitzgerald and William March. Colum's essay also identified the theme of humanistic sainthood which now, thanks largely to Maritain, dominated Callaghan's writing and thinking. Praising Callaghan's portrayal of Father Dowling, she wrote that "his gradual sinking into mental confusion, after an emotional upset and bewilderment at the injustice of the world, is done with such beauty and reality that the man remains as he was at the beginning, a kind of saint without weakness or milk-soppery" (51).

SAINTED TRIAD

"A saint without weakness or milksoppery." The phrase was prescient. Sainthood had long fascinated Maritain and, during those long winter evenings of 1933, no doubt had featured in the conversations. Essential to his and Callaghan's conception of a theocentric humanism, the saint was a type of anarchist, an individualist who acted humanistically against an inhumane society according to his or her own spiritual standards. A mixture of clown, outsider, and social criminal, the saint is an ambivalent character, one who operates in between official and unofficial discourse, searching always for a personally authentic truth. As Maritain himself remarked, "The saints always amaze us. Their virtues are freer than those of a merely virtuous man. Now and again, in circumstances outwardly alike, they act quite differently from the way in which a merely virtuous man acts. . . . They have their own kind of mean, their own kinds of standards. But they are valid only for each one of them" (*Existence and the Existent* 55).

Years later Callaghan would remark, with a large dollop of congenial irony,

There's a very thin borderline between innocence and crime. . . . the saint and the sinner, or the saint, let us say, and the man guilty of the sin of monstrous pride — there's a very thin line there because the saint in his own way has a kind of monstrous egotism. And the great criminal has a monstrous egotism. . . . [each] puts himself against the world and the laws of society. I haven't thought of this before. . . . ("Talk" 22)

But Callaghan thought of little else in the years following Maritain's visit. What is most remarkable in the great triad of novels published in 1934, 1935, and 1937 — *Such Is My Beloved, They Shall Inherit the Earth*, and *More Joy in Heaven* — is the fact that Callaghan now explored with unrelenting theological curiosity the intermingled and blurred boundaries between crime and sainthood. Sharing Maritain's interest in the possibility of a saint who lives spiritually under material conditions, he created, in both *They Shall Inherit the Earth* and *More Joy in Heaven*, allegories of resistant spiritual anarchism.

In both novels Callaghan explores the subtle moral contortions that necessarily arise when saints pit themselves against the power of social ideologies. And both books, like *Such Is My Beloved*, experiment formally with a type of moral allegory: the lone protagonist, an Everyman, confronts a constellation of symbolic characters who represent various social panaceas such as Marxism, doctrinaire religion, and astringent biological determinism. But like the earlier Father Dowling, both heroes reject the socially-sanctioned solution to moral dilemmas, opting instead for an individualistic, indeed anarchic, approach.

Callaghan's heroes in these novels, though uniquely portrayed, bear an uncanny resemblance to Maritain's theological construct: they are saints whose personal morality runs counter to the flimsy moralities of the social world. Although the biblically entitled books in the triad are not solely fictional renditions of theological premises, all do ultimately interweave with the thought of Jacques Maritain. The winter conversations on Avenue Road had left their incontrovertible mark. After Maritain, Callaghan would no longer present characters at the mercy of determining forces.

PRELUDE TO A DRY SPELL

Throughout the latter part of the thirties, as Callaghan was constructing his great triad, as he embarked on his spiritual adventure, he also had his fair share of leisure time. He and Loretto continued to fish and camp in Northern Ontario each summer, favouring the Georgian Bay area around Collingwood or the northern edges of Lake Superior. There were also visits to Josephine Herbst and John Herrmann, in Erwinna, Pennsylvania, as well as jolly trips to New York City.

Such small pleasures aside, though, the hard realities of the depression period continued to impinge on the Callaghans. Times were difficult on the financial front. Novel writing was a luxury that paid poorly — Callaghan needed to continue with the stories. Hardly as labour intensive as novel writing, stories simply sold more quickly and more regularly, putting much-needed food on the table. More ominously, Callaghan was experiencing the first cold twinges of an imminent artistic paralysis. Though the decade had had a spectacular start, as early as September 1934 Callaghan was already complaining to Perkins about his growing difficulty in finding new ideas (Letter to Perkins, 10 Sept. [1934]).

By April of 1934, *Such Is My Beloved* had sold only a thousand copies; plans to copublish in Britain with Hamish Hamilton had fallen through; and by late May, while in New York, Callaghan tried to negotiate with Scribner's a large advance on *They Shall Inherit the Earth*. But Scribner's, who had consistently done poorly with Callaghan's books, were unable to undertake such a contract. With great reluctance on Callaghan's part, and a genuine sadness on Perkins's, Callaghan switched publishers and accepted an advance of $2500 from Random House in February 1935.

The agreement gave the new publishers first rights on the current work-in-progress (most likely *They Shall Inherit the Earth*, which Callaghan had half completed) and a new collection of stories. Though *Inherit* would eventually appear with Macmillan, Random House was true to its word and brought out *Now That April's Here* in 1936 and *More Joy in Heaven* in 1937. But the enthusiasm of both author and publisher was destined to be short-lived.

On another professional front, Callaghan was disappointed at the failure of his application for a Guggenheim Fellowship in December 1935. Having been invited to apply by Henry Allen Moe, he had listed Sinclair Lewis, Donald Adams, Max Perkins, and the editors of the *New Yorker* as his referees. At home, he faced mounting financial obligations with the arrival of his second son, Barry, in July 1937. And as inflation ran rampant and unemployment became epidemic — 1.2 million Canadians were on relief by March 1937 — publishers began to cut back and conserve costs.

Although Callaghan continued to publish stories at an impressive rate until the end of 1938, they were beginning to evolve more slowly and had become progressively more difficult to sell. As the decade drew to a close, and as he became dispirited over political developments in Europe, Callaghan entered what he would later describe as "the dark period of my life" ("Talk" 20). Now he would begin to shift his emphasis away from the world of literature; he would explore a series of alternative careers to sustain him through his time of spiritual drought.

Of all that was happening in the world in the late thirties, most disheartening for Callaghan were the black clouds gathering over Europe. In July 1936, General Francisco Franco's fascists rose against the Republican government of Spain, claiming their actions were, amongst other things, a pious revolt against godless corruption. For Callaghan, as for many intellectuals of the time, such claims were pure bombast. Stating unequivocally that his was a "Christian point of view," he wrote in the leftist *New Frontier* that "[t]he spectacle of the devout foreign legion thugs and pious, infidel Moors, the ancient enemies of the Christian Spanish people marching to the tune of Onward Christian Soldiers leaves me very cold indeed" ("Where I Stand on Spain" 14). There was also the more pervasive prospect of another world war.

For Callaghan this inexorable slide into global violence was a nightmare. As he remarked years later in "The Pleasures of Failure," "The rise of Hitler and the Spanish war had made me profoundly cynical about the Great War that was approaching. For years I had been writing stories for *The New Yorker*. Suddenly I couldn't write such stories. Any story I attempted was done half-heartedly" (13). Callaghan's wry essay, written in 1965, provides a fascinating glimpse into this "period of spiritual dryness" ("Failure" 13), one of the grimmer phases of an otherwise glorious, multifaceted career.

Conditions on the home front were mixed. On one hand, Callaghan had a healthy and growing family which he enjoyed immensely (by 1939 Michael was eight and Barry only two). However, he now faced not only the invasive fears and insecurities of a wartime parent, but also paralyzing financial demands. More pragmatically, the wartime economy forced cutbacks in virtually all areas of social and cultural production. As publishers scurried to save costs and maximize output, experimental stories falling outside popular tastes became progressively more difficult to sell. By 1939 Callaghan was brought face to face with this new order: he failed to sell eight new stories in a row.

At this point Callaghan's hand was forced: "I was broke. I couldn't write anything anyone wanted to read" ("Failure" 13). In desperation he tried to borrow money; he tried to sell his car; he even considered returning to law. Nothing worked. After a few weeks of morbid depression, he realized that it was not so much failure as the incapacitating surrender to it that could cripple a human being. The trick was to acknowledge that "failures are often more interesting than successes. They can toughen your spirit" ("Failure" 12).

With this conviction, and "[a]ccepting the fact that [he] couldn't write stories in this period," Callaghan jettisoned his apathy and determinedly "turned to something else" ("Failure" 13). What he turned to was a fascinating series of extraordinarily successful failures. For all intents and purposes, he now abandoned his principal career as a novelist and storyteller, and for the next twelve years, from 1938 until 1950, he travelled almost incessantly, working as a dramatist in New York, a journalist in Toronto, a screenwriter in Halifax, and as a cross-Canada radio host.

In each of these new roles, however populist they may have been, however much a failure they may have seemed to him at the time, Callaghan managed to salvage something of significance. He remained to the end a dedicated wordsmith, an aspiring saint engaged in artistic and personal struggle. Meandering as perhaps they were, these "failures" proved later to be an extraordinary success, for Callaghan's experiences during this twelve-year hiatus would form the architectural scaffolding of some of his greatest writing. As he remarked in "The Pleasures of Failure," "There wasn't a time when I wasn't thinking about writing" (37). All was grist to the mill.

DRAMATIC WORK

Initially, Callaghan's short-lived career as a dramatist was decidedly mercenary. Desperately needing money in the summer of

FIGURE 5

Callaghan (right) as CBC *radio host, with John Fisher.*

1938, he "took out an old play that had once aroused some interest in New York, borrowed money on an insurance policy, and went to work" ("Failure" 13). This script, entitled first "Turn Again Home" then later *Going Home*, was an adaptation of *They Shall Inherit the Earth*, a project suggested by Lawrence Langner of the New York Theatre Guild. Divided into three acts, the play is a distillation of the novel's father-son theme and concentrates on the estrangement and ultimate reconciliation of Michael Aikenhead and his father, Andrew. Though much of the novel's rich embroidery is necessarily pared down to meet the requirements of the stage, the central plot still turns upon the not-so-accidental drowning of Dave Choate.

By late 1939, Langner took an option on the script and Callaghan was paid advance royalties. In a mood of heady optimism Callaghan travelled to New York and Connecticut, making minor revisions to the script along the way. Callaghan auditioned actors with Langner, socialized with the American writer and dramatist William Saroyan, and confidently looked forward to fame and fortune. By January 1940, the play was in full rehearsal and the entire project seemed destined to be a spectacular success.

But failure seemed to dog Callaghan's every move. The actors they auditioned were rejected: Langner vetoed Callaghan's top choices. Though Callaghan and Langner got on famously, at one point they argued violently when Callaghan suggested Britain would surely lose the war unless the United States came to her aid. Moreover, because of the guild's straitened finances, Langner and his coproducers felt it imperative to secure guaranteed drawing cards for the main roles and tried vainly to hire high-profile Hollywood actors. All attempts failed in the long run. What with impossible casting problems, mounting personal tensions between playwright and producers, and growing financial difficulties, Callaghan's play was finally dropped in the early part of 1941.

This failure notwithstanding, Callaghan remained optimistic: he had one more theatrical ace up his dramatist's sleeve. Buoyed in the first instance by Langner's interest, he had begun another play in late 1939, "Just Ask for George," finishing it on 8 May 1940 (Letter to McAfee, 8 May [1940]). This was a symbolic drama in which a young Canadian sailor, George, finds himself down on his luck after being discharged from the navy. He travels to the United States, works in a cheap New York–state beanery, and settles down to seek the "truth" of North American culture.

Uncomfortably similar to William Saroyan's 1939 *The Time of Your Life*, "Just Ask for George" was characterized, like *Strange Fugitive*, by a hard-boiled study of character, tough-sounding dialogue, and plenty of ironic contrasts between the hero's fantasy life and the grim realities that surround him. Really a drama of ideas, the script was readily picked up by two young producers, Curtis and Blackwell, who not only immediately assigned a director and began casting, but who also, more crucially, paid Callaghan an advance.

Once again, however, bad luck and spectral serendipity came into play. Within months Curtis and Blackwell became curiously out of touch; although Callaghan read advertisements for his upcoming play in the New York papers, he heard nothing of current developments. With mounting anxiety he travelled overnight to New York, only to learn from his producers that "Just Ask for George," like *Going Home*, had been cancelled. The main reason, Callaghan wrote, was that "one of the principal backers, just before putting up the money, had got drunk and boarded a plane for the west coast, and his wife, having tracked him down, had had him committed to a sanatorium as an alcoholic, and, of course, had cancelled his investment in [the] play" ("Failure" 34).

Most people would have been distraught at this turn of events. After failing to sell his stories, Callaghan had turned to the theatre as a desperate last-ditch effort to support his family through creative writing. Now he had to return from New York to face his friends and creditors — as well as Loretto, Michael, and Barry — and explain that two years of work had come to nought. More importantly, he would have to announce that there would be no income from the plays.

It is a mark of Callaghan's resilience, what was really his

extraordinarily tough-minded spirit, that at this point he "felt no real panic at all." As he recalled in "The Pleasures of Failure":

> I was accepting the failure as a normal part of my life. I was becoming aware that there might be other times that would be like little deaths, dreadful depressions, but if I didn't get to like these deaths — that's the great trick: not to have a secret liking for them so you court them as some men do — then the spark in the spirit would flame again just because I very much wanted to remain alive. (37)

The plays had been an experiment and the experiment had failed. Although hindsight has shown that the work was not a total loss — the plays would reappear in altered form in subsequent novels — at the time there was little comfort.[5] At this point the wolf was still at the door; Callaghan would have to turn to something else. And he did so with uncommon gusto.

RETURN TO JOURNALISM

Having a hunch that he still "wasn't ready" to resume storytelling ("Failure" 37), Callaghan returned to his first port of call: the brassy, hustling world of popular journalism. The move was hardly a surprise. Not only had he accumulated considerable experience at the *Star* in the twenties, but while investing his energies with the New York Theatre Guild, Callaghan had been slowly building a reputation in Toronto as the tough reviewer and uncompromising columnist for *Saturday Night*. By 1940 he had already reviewed Faulkner, Steinbeck, Joyce, Dos Passos, Wolfe, and Richard Wright. He had also critically addressed such contemporary issues as the rise of fascism in Europe; the — in his view — seductive and false allure of Marxism; the role of artistic genius within the state. Such early beginnings pointed directly to what were now to become Callaghan's principal preoccupations.

Callaghan's reviews provide an unerring guide to his own writerly ideals. Like Lawrence's *Studies in Classic American Liter-*

ature or Leacock's criticism of Dickens, Callaghan's critical evaluations emerge as indirect theoretical and critical statements about his own literary values. For example, he lavishly praised Steinbeck's *The Grapes of Wrath* for its realistic and unselfconscious presentation of life, yet faulted its didactic diatribes and selfconscious exhortations. More often than not, Callaghan's evaluations were hard-hitting and direct. Even in his reviews he was the pugilist.

But Callaghan was no narcissistic drudge, blindly reading his own values into others' texts. On the contrary, his reviews often disclose an enthusiastic response to new and experimental methods. For example, James Joyce, whose writings are most different from Callaghan's, is applauded for *Finnegans Wake*, though Callaghan feels "the dream form or anti-logical structure is frequently employed simply as a structure for the prose ballet." Nonetheless, he defends the right of "a great master . . . going his own way" and praises Joyce's vitality and linguistic versatility ("Into the Dream World" 21).

Callaghan's reviews reveal a mind continually growing and changing in its confrontation with other writers, a mind quietly adding to its own store. By reviewing such diverse writers, Callaghan wasn't merely putting bread on the table; he was, however indirectly, continuing to hone his present aesthetic theories for future use.

Though Callaghan continued to review intermittently for *Saturday Night* until 1942 (and once for *Canadian Forum* in 1940), his principal journalistic writings, from 1940 until 1950, included a vast series of commentaries, political columns, sports profiles, and human interest stories. He first began writing the columns while at *Saturday Night*, but developed them most fully after he joined E.P. Taylor's fledgling magazine, *New World Illustrated*, in March 1940, the same year he joined the Civil Liberties Union. Edited by J.K. Thomas — who, with his wife, Hallie, would remain Callaghan's lifelong friend — the magazine lasted until 1948 when it was absorbed by the *National Home Monthly*, with which Callaghan remained for two more years until February 1950.

In its first year, *New World* had an international board of contributors, including Callaghan and Mary Lowrey Ross from Ontario; Graham McInnes from London; and Harland Manchester from New York. It offered a general coverage of news, sports, current events, arts, and entertainment, not unlike the mediocre *mélanges* of today's *Maclean's* or *Time* magazines.

Initially Callaghan worked exclusively as a sports commentator, producing congenial, jocular profiles on hockey, baseball, wrestling, horse racing, and golf — not to mention an amusing story on the impossible vagaries of cricket. He developed a close friendship with Dink Carroll, the Montreal sports writer whom he would subsequently visit throughout the forties and fifties, attending hockey games at the Montreal Forum. After only a few months, Callaghan branched out: until 1950, he produced over seventy monthly columns that covered everything from soup to nuts, from the ideological limitations of Marxism to the changing trends in women's fashions.[6] The complex significance of this body of popular writing cannot be overemphasized.

In one sense Callaghan's journalism, like his two plays, was simply and straightforwardly a money-making gambit. Times were tough; he had young children to support; he was good with words; he became a journalist. In this limited sense, the columns show how well he had learned his lessons at the *Star*. A model of their kind, they are the product of a newsman's pen: detached, occasionally humorous pieces of hard news.

But the columns are also more, much more, than this. What so distinctively marks many of Callaghan's columns for *Saturday Night*, *New World*, and later the *National Home Monthly* is their singular literariness, the unwavering intellectualism that underpins the more argumentative and analytic political pieces. Whereas many of these profiles are ostensibly straightforward commentaries — which more often than not take a left-of-centre, vaguely individualist position — they often contain a brief narrative marked by controlled irony, extended metaphor, colloquial dialogue, and the kernel of a fully-blown novelistic narrative. Callaghan's was no tabloid journalism; his journalistic prose was highly stylized, designed from the start to sway, entice, and subject his readers.

Even more important than Callaghan's stylistic modulations is the fact that so many of his columns would later become grist for his novelistic mill. At the simplest level, many of the columns came to function as a first draft of a later story, providing a basic plot, a kernel of dialogue, or an embryonic situation. Even the sports columns bob up in Callaghan's later portrayals of the hockey game in *The Loved and the Lost* and of the boxer, Mike Kon, who appears in *The Many Colored Coat*.

Most intriguing is how at this time Callaghan was tentatively beginning to work through the ideas, issues, and moral conundrums that he would later incorporate into his fiction. Many of his columns, however populist, address ideas about Canadian puritanism, utilitarianism, Canadian nationalism, legal censorship, and Christian personalism — all themes that would underpin such works as *Luke Baldwin's Vow*, *The Varsity Story*, and "The Man with the Coat."

The point, the most crucial point of all, is that while much of the journalism Callaghan churned out during the forties was money-spinning stuff, most of it was not. On the contrary, Callaghan's second journalistic career constituted a critically transformative phase in his development as a novelist and thinker. Both in terms of stylistic versatility and intellectual refinement, these columns formed the architectural base of what would emerge throughout the fifties and early sixties as Callaghan's particular and personal variety of fiction. As a man, Callaghan hardened and toughened in the brassy world of forties journalism; as a writer, his talent underwent a modulating, strangely fluid transmutation.

ON BOARD WITH JORIS IVENS

One of the principal factors in Callaghan's later novelistic development was his often overlooked media career, what was really a series of jobs that overlapped with each other and with his journalism. Beginning in 1942, while still writing his monthly column for *New World Illustrated*, Callaghan lived the life of a screenwriter, radio host, and television personality.

A sense of the depression underlying Callaghan's feverish activity in these years can be gleaned from one of Loretto Callaghan's rare surviving letters. In a Christmas card to Josephine Herbst, probably written in 1943, she wrote,

> [Morley] is away touring Canada on a postwar program called "Of Things to Come." I think one of the reasons he didn't write was that he had become terribly discouraged about his writing — after spending so much time on the theatre nothing came of it — and then he couldn't seem to get back into stride writing anything else. One summer he took a job with the Canadian Film Corporation, writing the script for a movie short of the Canadian navy and had some experience sailing around the Atlantic and now he is sailing around the land on this broadcast job. Maybe one of these days when he gets tired of it all, or the war is over, or something, he will settle down and write again. (Letter to Herbst, [Dec. 1943])

Though Callaghan felt that these media jobs involved his "peripheral talents" rather than his "central talent" (Callaghan, "Talk" 19), he did them, if not begrudgingly, then with a certain mixture of worn-out resignation and muted optimism. As he wryly remarked to Robert Weaver in 1958, "You do all kinds of wild things in your life. I may conduct myself on several fronts. A man ought to. . . . Why did I do other things? Well, mainly because people asked me to, and the flesh is weak . . ." ("Talk" 19–20).

One of the things Callaghan was asked to do in 1942 was to write a script about Canada's wartime navy for the National Film Board. He already had some screen-writing experience, having written a commentary in 1940 for Irving Jacoby's twenty-one-minute hockey film, *Hot Ice*.[7] Now, in 1942, when his literary output was confined to seeing his story "The Two Fishermen" anthologized in Whit Burnett's Dial Press Anthology, Callaghan became script consultant for the well-known film director Joris Ivens and travelled between Ottawa and Halifax for the summer. His task was to evolve a workable script for a film to be entitled *Action Stations*, which the navy had commissioned as a piece of patriotic propaganda.

Of all Callaghan's media experiences, this is the most overlooked and undervalued, since the script lay undiscovered in the NFB Archives until 1991. The received opinion is that Callaghan went to sea with Ivens, wrote the script, then "resigned in despair over the extensive production complications" (Latham 22). But from Callaghan's manuscript and his two letters to John Grierson, then director of the NFB, we now know the more complicated, typically agonistic truth of Callaghan's filmic involvement.

In a letter to Grierson dated 17 August 1942, Callaghan outlined the comedy of errors that had led not only to his initial involvement in the project, but also to his final departure from it. When he first came on board — at whose invitation is uncertain — Joris Ivens already possessed a script that had been previously approved by both the navy and the NFB. This script showed the historical development of Canada's naval forces and celebrated their present involvement in running convoys from Halifax to Londonderry. It called for a three-part film, which would include a ridiculous cartoon interval with Popeye the Sailor commenting on the growth of the navy. Needless to say, Callaghan and Ivens were both horrified, and together they discussed the possibility of a more adult-oriented script centred upon a Canadian corvette that would hunt and destroy a German U-boat. After their discussion, Ivens set out to sea and shot the submarine sequence, fully intending to integrate more footage of burning ships and ocean storms from the NFB's own naval archives.

The film shoot completed, Callaghan suggested abandoning the official script. With Ivens's approval, they set to work for two weeks, "busier than hell," to revamp the script and centre it on the submarine plot-line (Letter to Grierson, 17 Aug. [1942]). Callaghan also tried to incorporate a more humane angle, concentrating on character development and including individual traits of the sailors involved. Accordingly, his script contains detailed thumbnail sketches of individual sailors. One significant scene involves a bosun who saves a man's life by undressing and warming the frozen victim with his own body heat. This scene would appear virtually unchanged over thirty-five years later in *Close to the Sun Again* (71–72), Callaghan's novel about Ira Groome, former commander of a Canadian wartime corvette. Groome's prototype can also be detected in the script: one of the central figures is that of "The Old Man," the commander who resembles a fatherly version of Captain Ahab (indeed, he thinks of hidden submarines as versions of the white whale, Moby Dick). In short, the script outlines a tense voyage across the Atlantic, during which the corvette rescues four drifting survivors and sinks a German submarine. Exhausted but triumphant, the Canadians at last arrive heroically in Londonderry.

The fate of Callaghan's script in 1942 was a mysterious, almost uncanny repetition of his experiences with the New York Theatre Guild. According to Callaghan's angry letters to Grierson, both he and Ivens were stopped, involuntarily, in mid-production. As Callaghan complained to Grierson, "As a result of my democratic experiences in Halifax I . . . was left dangling sedately way out on the end of a limb" (Letter to Grierson, 17 Aug. [1942]).

The reason for the film's termination was never fully explained. To Grierson, Callaghan ironically alludes to suggestions that the project, gone well over-budget, was considered by the NFB a waste of taxpayers' money. More likely is that there was considerable confusion and irritation at the NFB about Callaghan's role as script consultant. Callaghan had felt that he was free to revise the script, but both the NFB and the navy, who had already approved one version and expected Ivens to follow through with that, disagreed. Whatever the explanation, the result of the confusion was that the project was temporarily halted. Though Ivens did eventually complete a version of *Action Stations*, it was neither the officially sanctioned original script nor Callaghan's twenty-six-page version.

CALLAGHAN AS RADIO HOST

Though Callaghan would later joke to Josephine Herbst that "during the war I spent a whole summer with the navy sailing out of Halifax with the convoys [and was] a great adventurer, a lover of action, a fearless fighter, [and] a reckless fellow who mastered the briny deep" (Letter to Herbst, 20 Jan. [1948]), he was also, less glamorously, a radio host for most of the decade. After the NFB fiasco at the end of the summer of 1942, he returned from Halifax to Toronto and, at the invitation of the Canadian Broadcasting Corporation, began in 1943 what would become a forty-year relationship with CBC Radio and Television.

At first he was a panel member on the radio show, *Of Things to Come: Inquiry into the Post-War World*. This was a monthly half-hour current events programme, later called *Citizen's Forum*, with which Callaghan was associated until 1947. According to Brandon Conron, "[i]ts controversial discussions are credited with stimulating the establishment of a library in one town, a juvenile court in another, and with focusing attention on such thorny questions as fair employment practices" (*Morley Callaghan* [1966] 122). In his role as "Counsel of the People," a role pre-eminently suited to Callaghan given his earlier legal training, Callaghan was continually on the road. These frequent travels across Canada led him to view the country in a new light. As he remarked to Robert Weaver, "I don't know whether to look back with bitterness or hope on this period, but in those ten years, God forgive me, I began to take a great interest in Canada" ("Talk" 20).

A growing nationalist interest underlay a number of Callaghan's decisions at this time. Following *Of Things to Come*, he rejected a Hollywood offer to write a promotional novel for the

Bing Crosby film *Going My Way* (Latham 22), opting instead to chair such controversial CBC Radio issues programmes as *The Farmer's Future, Who Shapes the Future?*, and *Action Now: How the People Can Make their Power Felt*. In 1947 he briefly joined the new CBC Radio quiz show *Beat the Champs*. But at this point Callaghan's world was beginning to change yet again. Within this maelstrom of activity, new possibilities, some bright, some dark, were percolating.

FAMILY TRAGEDY TO PERSONAL REBIRTH

In the five years following the war, Callaghan lost three beloved family members: his brother Burke — who by this point had embarked on a promising operatic career — died unexpectedly in 1946. This loss was soon followed on 6 December 1948 by the death of his seventy-six-year-old father, Thomas, who had suffered a painful gastric haemorrhage on Christmas Day the year before (Letter to Herbst, [Dec. 1949]). Just two years later, in 1950, his mother, Mary, died on 28 December at the age of eighty.

Strangely, almost spiritually, these losses seem to have revived Callaghan's creative instincts. Although he had published a sprinkling of stories during the war — most notably, "Very Special Shoes" in 1943 — after 1946 he began again to write in earnest. By 1950 he had sold a dozen stories to such magazines as the *Saturday Evening Post*, the *American Magazine, Maclean's*, and *Mademoiselle*; in 1948 he published the promotional novel *The Varsity Story* for the University of Toronto; the New Play Society staged *To Tell the Truth* to critical acclaim in 1949;[8] and in 1950 *Going Home* was featured at the Royal Ontario Museum Theatre.[9] More importantly, there was now renewed critical interest in his work. Once again Morley Callaghan was becoming recognized as a writer rather than as a media personality.

Most significantly at this time, soon after his father's death in 1948, Callaghan undertook a curiously symbolic project: he expanded his 1947 *Saturday Evening Post* story of a recently orphaned boy, "Luke Baldwin's Vow," into an adolescent novel with the same title. In this novel the orphaned Luke Baldwin recovers from the death of his father, in the process discovering the limitations of a utilitarian worldview. Luke must learn the value and necessity of a creative imagination, but in order to acquire this knowledge, he must first beat the utilitarians at their own game. In an echo of Callaghan's recent predicaments, Luke vows "that he would always have some money on hand, no matter what became of him, so that he would be able to protect all that was truly valuable from the practical people in the world" (*Luke Baldwin's Vow* 187).

In writing of Luke's spiritual yet materially-aware rebirth, Callaghan was unconsciously charting the directions of his own writerly resurrection. Like his child-orphan hero, he had experienced material want; now that he had survived, he would return to what was truly valuable to him: the sainted dedication to authenticity and imaginative creation.

As the decade drew to a close, Callaghan limited his use of "peripheral talents." Although he would continue his radio and television work for the CBC, and would write intermittent reviews and columns, he was preparing for something substantially more momentous. After the appearance of *Luke Baldwin's Vow* towards the end of 1948, he abandoned the fragments of his wartime work-in-progress — what would years later become *Close to the Sun Again* — and started on the novel that would earn him his first Governor General's Award for Fiction: *The Loved and the Lost*. The period of spiritual drought had come to an end.

THE SPARK IN THE SPIRIT

In January 1938, Callaghan wrote a strong and angry piece for the *University of Toronto Quarterly*. Entitled "The Plight of Canadian Fiction," the essay was a ferocious broadside against popular writing, the kind of easy entertainment that Callaghan felt was dominating Canadian writing at this time. The essay anticipates many of his later criticisms of Sinclair Lewis in *That Summer in Paris*: the true writer must challenge, not divert, the reader; the writer must force the reader to struggle uncomfortably with his or her unique and personal point of view.

Like Jacques Maritain's ideal saint or anarchist, in other words, the authentic artist acts according to standards and must "look at reality with his [or her] own eyes . . ." ("Plight" 155). The struggle between writer and reader thus constitutes for Callaghan a spiritual exercise, in which the text becomes a potential site of profound moral and intellectual transformation for the reader.

Now, at the close of the forties, when Callaghan looked back over the past decade, he felt a mixture of guilt and exultation. True enough, he had often capitulated to material exigencies: in many of his columns and broadcasts he had indeed pandered to audience demands for diversion. He realized, then, that he had often wandered from the true path of novelistic sainthood. As he wrote in a Christmas card to Josephine Herbst — who herself had recently experienced a severe writer's block — "I suffer, I suppose, from what the boys call 'guilt feelings' " (Letter to Herbst, [Dec. 1949]).

But there was also exultation, an optimistic faith in what Herbst, in her reply, called "some curious kind of equilibrium that certainly has not depended upon electric dishwashers, new model cars or elegant clothes; these I have not had and don't give a damn" (Letter to Callaghan, 28 Dec. [1949]). In Canada the postwar period was one of rapid economic recovery: publishers once again sought out stories. The financial hardships of the past ten years began to lessen, and now, at the turn of the decade, Callaghan could finally return to what he did best. Like Herbst, he firmly believed that "there are other levels to be sought; the new colonies are probably of the mind that we still know so little about" (Herbst, Letter to Callaghan, 28 Dec. [1949]). For the next quarter-century, beginning with *The Loved and the Lost* — his controversial story of sexuality, murder, and betrayal — Callaghan would wondrously explore these "new colonies."

Outwardly, Callaghan's life acquired all the semblances of quiet conservativism, even semiretirement. He was now in his late forties, that period when older friends and mentors begin to die. As the decade opened, the Callaghans were saddened by the passing of E.K. Brown in 1951, a close family friend and former editor of the *University of Toronto Quarterly*. As Loretto gently wrote to Peggy Brown, "Morley and I take your hand and say we are very very sorry" (Letter to Brown, 8 May 1951).

But despite their melancholy over the loss of their friend, the Callaghans were generally in congenial spirits at this time, for they had at last decided to settle down. In 1952, after many years of renting at Walmer Road, Callaghan and Loretto purchased their stately Rosedale home at 20 Dale Avenue where they would reside permanently. This domestic security was matched by long-sought financial solvency: in 1952 Callaghan was awarded the Governor General's Award for *The Loved and the Lost*, a book which he nonetheless felt had been "stupidly read" (Callaghan, "Talk" 24). In following years he would receive a number of highly remunerative awards, most notable among them the $5000 *Maclean's* Fiction Prize in 1955 for "The Man with the Coat."

There was, moreover, an increasingly sympathetic critical industry slowly building around Callaghan's *oeuvre*. Whereas the early reviewers had hailed him as a hard-boiled disciple of Hemingway, he was now slowly emerging in critical discussions as an overlooked novelist-philosopher, a writer whose ideas constituted a profoundly searching analysis of the modern age. Although Desmond Pacey's ground-breaking *Creative Writing in Canada* accused Callaghan of moral flabbiness, by the late fifties critics such as Malcolm Ross, Hugo McPherson, and F.W. Watt all began to emphasize his spiritual depth, intellectual rigour, and critical acumen. These revisions of Callaghan's reputation reached their apogee in 1960 when the leading American critic, Edmund Wilson, proffered his by now famous evaluation: that Morley Callaghan was "perhaps the most unjustly neglected novelist in the English-speaking world," a writer whose works "may be mentioned without absurdity in association with Chekhov's and Turgenev's . . ." (106, 113).

Against this progressively secure and increasingly prestigious backdrop, Callaghan's intellectual life took on an intensified, anarchic, and highly controversial character. Like the plays of the German playwright Bertolt Brecht, Callaghan's writing turned to the underworld existing alongside respectable society; once again he exhibited a fascination with sinners, social misfits, boxers, prostitutes, and crooks. And though *The Loved and the Lost* had continued his characteristic moral enquiry into the ambiguous meanings of truth, he now began to write with an even greater intellectual elasticity and philosophical resilience.

Innocence, that great overarching concern of his religious trilogy, was now evolving into a conceptual framework based on the collapse of moral absolutes and the cherishing of mixed categories. As Callaghan remarked to Robert Weaver in 1958,

I am bored by pure innocence. I don't know any pure innocents. . . . A man's nature is a very tangled web, shot through with gleams of heavenly light, no doubt, and the darkness of what we call evil forces. And the great trick, I suppose, is to remain on an even keel — and somehow or other be able to draw yourself together and realize your potentialities as a man. And the great sin really is to not realize your own possibilities. ("Talk" 23)

From 1952 onwards, Callaghan would retain this "even keel," quietly and surely working at a series of interlocking occupations. Whereas the forties had been marked by a variety of discrete jobs that occasionally overlapped, his various activities now melded more seamlessly, interconnecting in a series of continuous and usually abrasive confrontations with established opinion. The brash young boxer of the twenties and thirties, the hustler of the forties, now settled in as an intellectual colonizer of the mind.

Callaghan found himself within a virtual whirlwind of activity in the 1950s. After winning the Governor General's Award in 1952, he wrote some of his finest stories — including "Magic Hat" and "A Cap for Steve" — and in 1953 began work on a long novella, "The Man with the Coat" — a story which, like *They Shall Inherit the Earth*, explores the limits and liabilities of public, as opposed to private, guilt. Callaghan was also becoming increasingly active as a literary critic: in 1954 his *New World* column on Toronto was reprinted in Malcolm Ross's *Our Sense of Identity*, and soon after this, in October 1955, he travelled to Kingston to deliver a lecture on the novelist's craft for the Canadian Writers' Conference.

To many Canadians throughout the fifties and sixties, Callaghan was best known, first as the abrasive guest on CBC Television's *Fighting Words*, and second, as the feisty panellist on CBC Radio's cultural affairs programme, *Now I Ask You*, and the lyrical contributor to CBC's literary programme, *Anthology*. Obvious money-makers, these peripheral activities nonetheless brought him into continuous contact with a broad cultural spectrum.

In each of these programmes Callaghan was always the pugilist, a tough-minded participant who regularly ran against popular taste. He was renowned for his blunt opinions — on everything from Canadian writing to censorship — and his even blunter manner of stating them. Drawing on his early training as a debater and lawyer — and partly as a boxer — he rarely adopted conventional notions, more often than not debating, with considerable finesse, the finer points of moral conundrums such as public opinions about premarital sex or literary problems connected with contemporary experimental writing in Canada. In these programmes Callaghan was brought into contact — and occasional conflict — with such personalities as Nathan Cohen, Joyce Davidson, and Percy Saltzman. From this point onward he was also in sporadic correspondence with Canadian writers as diverse as Hugh Hood, Earle Birney, Margaret Laurence, and Mordecai Richler.

Callaghan appeared as a regular panellist on *Fighting Words* from 1955 until 1961; he appeared on *Now I Ask You* twice in 1964 and twice in 1966. But simultaneously, as CBC Radio's *Of Things to Come* was cancelled, Callaghan began what was to become a twenty-eight year literary commitment with CBC Radio. He had two brief stints in 1955 and 1956 on the literary programme, *Anthology*, during which he spoke on Canadian writing and theatre with Malcolm Ross, A.J.M. Smith, Douglas Campbell, and Mavor Moore. In 1957, the year he first met Edmund Wilson, Callaghan also began a series of readings from his own short fiction: during 1957 he read three stories on CBC's *Wednesday Night*; this series of readings then continued intermittently on *Anthology* from December 1957 until July 1972. But Callaghan also appeared on *Anthology* as both a literary and cultural critic, again intermittently, from 1959 until 1983. He began initially as a discussant on 1 May 1959, talking about book publishing in Canada with Robert Weaver and Jack McClelland. After spending most of the sixties as a reader of his own stories on *Anthology*, he resumed his critical role in January 1970 when *Anthology* began its monthly discussion series, "Books and Bookmen." As the principal guest — from January 1970 until May 1983 — Callaghan not only profiled the most recent national and international publications, but he also offered in-depth critical analyses of writers such as Samuel Beckett, John Dos Passos, Alexander Solzhenitsyn, and James T. Farrell.

PERSONAL ANARCHISMS

What makes Callaghan's media work of this period so important is the fact that it provides a fluid record of his ever-evolving, though paradoxically consistent, personal and literary principles throughout the fifties. In these discussions Callaghan covered a wide variety of topics: the role of the Canada Council, the value of contemporary writing, the importance of experimentalism in the work of Beckett and Pinter, or the nature of his own creative process.

Again and again, Callaghan returned almost compulsively to one overarching theme: the subversion of official ideologies and laws. As Brandon Conron has remarked, there was an intense animus in Callaghan towards the police, the law — in fact towards all forms of authority (Personal interview 1991). In these programmes Callaghan publicly developed an anarchic position, which valued above all else the primacy of the individual and asserted the individual's obligation to remain as true as possible to him- or herself. Whether Callaghan developed this position by way of his relationship with such left-wing thinkers and writers as Maritain and Josephine Herbst is moot; what is apparent is that during the period of McCarthyism in the United States and increased official surveillance in Canada, he began to articulate what would later become an openly anarchic response to officialdom.

Callaghan's tough-minded individualism became increasingly obvious in the novels: both *The Many Colored Coat*, which was itself a radical revision of "The Man with the Coat," and *A Passion in Rome*, with its vaguely blasphemous intermingling of sacred passion and earthy sexuality, openly taunted the oleaginous anxieties of Canadian puritanism. But it was in his journalistic columns for *Saturday Night* and *Maclean's* — which he wrote on and off from June 1951 until January 1960 — that Callaghan most abrasively confronted middle-class social and moral conservatism. In these pieces he persistently interrogated the mystified religious sources of Canadian puritanism, dismantling the delimiting structures of the conservative ethic.

Callaghan's left-of-centre thoughts on sexuality, censorship, and blasphemy, which would reappear in such "heretical" works as *Close to the Sun Again*, *A Time for Judas*, and *Our Lady of the Snows*, overlapped, in the late fifties, with a number of intriguing events. The 1959–60 obscenity trial of D.H. Lawrence's *Lady Chatterley's Lover* in the United States galvanized Callaghan. His January 1960 *Maclean's* article, "Why Single Out Sex as the Only

Real Road to Sin?", is a witty and outspoken elaboration of Callaghan's defence of Lawrence, a broadside against the popular tendency to see sexuality as "the root of all immorality" (6). The *Maclean's* essay rearticulates Callaghan's earlier frank treatments of sex in such works as *No Man's Meat*, *The Loved and the Lost*, and especially *The Many Colored Coat*.

Interestingly, Callaghan's *Maclean's* piece followed soon after his 1958 assignment for the *Star Weekly*, when he travelled to Rome to cover the death of Pope Pius xii. At that time he began drafting a novel set in Italy in which Catholicism would play a major role. Now, in 1960, he began to draw together the various threads, weaving them together to produce *A Passion in Rome*, a controversial novel because of its grand, almost neo-Lawrentian treatment of sexual love.

On one hand the novel attests to Callaghan's increasing impatience with middle-class morality; more importantly, in its celebration of a divine sexuality and a sexualized divinity, it shows him moving directly towards a celebration of a distinctly subversive individualism. Though the book would outrage some critics and bore others, *A Passion in Rome* marks a critical point in Callaghan's developing defence of the individual's obligation to realize, without fear, the full range of his or her potential, a potential that Callaghan himself was beginning to explore.

PUBLIC ACCLAIM

As the fifties drew to a close, Callaghan began to enjoy the fruits of his many labours. In 1957, his stories were attracting the interest of film-makers: that year Norman Klenman adapted "Silk Stockings," "Rocking Chair," "A Sick Call," and "The Rejected One" for William Davidson's short 1958 feature, *Now that April's Here*, for which Callaghan was paid $5000. According to Klenman, "Morley came on set often to watch. . . . [but] made no demands. He never talked about his stories, or the casting, the screenplay or the production. When Bill [Davidson] or I, as

FIGURE 6

The academic honours begin to roll in: Callaghan (right) receiving his honorary LLD *at the University of Western Ontario, 1965.*

co-producers, asked his advice he gave it to us, simply and succinctly." Though the film was a disaster both at the box office and with the critics, Davidson and Klenman initiated what, in the following years, would become something of a miniature industry in creating filmic adaptations of Callaghan's work.

Other accolades were in the wind. In 1958 Callaghan was offered the editorship of *Saturday Night*, a post he rejected; in 1959 Macmillan published the justly famous retrospective collection, *Morley Callaghan's Stories*. In the next few years, awards began to pile up. Callaghan received the Lorne Pierce Medal for Literature from the Royal Society in 1960; that same year he was named "Celebrity of the Day" by Celebrities International of New York. In 1961, after a virtual lifetime of neglect in his own city, Toronto awarded him the Civic Award of Merit. Callaghan could finally, after over thirty years of writing, bask in the glow of public recognition.

But he didn't. In December 1957, Robert Weaver conducted what is now considered to be one of the most important interviews with Callaghan, published the following spring in the *Tamarack Review*. In this wide-ranging, retrospective discussion, Callaghan offers succinct, blunt commentaries, not only on his ideas and writing career, but also on his present state of introspective solitude. At one point he balks at Weaver's question, "Do you want to talk about James Joyce, Scott Fitzgerald, and the others?", suggesting that he may write a memoir about those days in Paris (12). Yet earlier, at a more crucial point, he remarked with only a hint of irony:

> literature is a kind of muddied stream. As you grow older, you read more and more, and you get interested in the way other writers write, and you get interested in problems of writing, and you get interested in the way other writers see things. And in the course of time, especially if you're fond of reading as I am fond of reading, this begins to make writing more difficult. You become aware of problems that never existed as problems before. . . . Because the eyes of a

hundred other writers are in your way. You have a tendency to pick up their glasses and put them on. ("Talk" 4–5)

Callaghan's comments anticipated later developments. Even while writing *A Passion in Rome*, Callaghan was planning his own introspective retrospective, undergoing a process of looking inward, not only at the forces and friends who had populated his history, but at the influences that were now hindering his vision. One result of this meditative introspection was his famous memoir, *That Summer in Paris*, published in 1963. Callaghan would also, in the early sixties, begin a string of self-reflexive drafts, which he would continue to write and rewrite until his death thirty years later. As this phase of his "glorious career" came to a close, Callaghan began ever so slowly to examine the nature and significance of his own lifetime of writing.

LIFE AFTER *PARIS*

Following the New York launching of *That Summer in Paris*, when he once again met up with his dear friend, Josephine Herbst, Callaghan's life took a series of turns which he would find both exhilarating and devastating. Within the Canadian academy he began to receive critical and personal accolades. In 1965, through the agency of Brandon Conron, one of Callaghan's first major critics and now his friend, he was awarded an honorary Doctor of Letters by the University of Western Ontario, an honour followed the year after by an LL.D. from the University of Toronto. In 1972 he accepted an offer to be writer-in-residence at the University of Windsor, which awarded him yet another honorary degree, a D.Litt., in 1973.

Alongside these academic kudos, which Callaghan beheld with something of an amused eye, he received the Canada Council Medal in 1966. True to form, however, one year later he contemptuously rejected the offer of the Medal of Service of the Order of Canada, arguing that it was a second-class honour in comparison to the Companion Medal earlier awarded to Hugh

FIGURE 7

Callaghan with his ever-present pipe, 1970.

MacLennan. Finally, in 1982, he graciously accepted the Companion Medal from Prime Minister Pierre Trudeau, who privately apologized for his predecessor's oversight.

Throughout the late sixties and seventies, such critics as Brandon Conron, George Woodcock, Victor Hoar, David Staines, and Patricia Morley were devoting much critical attention to Callaghan's work. This "validation" by the literary academy culminated in 1980 when the University of Ottawa hosted a critical symposium in his honour. More financially rewarding were the $15,000 Molson Prize and the $50,000 Royal Bank Award in 1970. These awards allowed Callaghan to undertake less sustenance work — work such as book reviewing, which admittedly he continued sporadically — and concentrate on the series of novels that would occupy him throughout the seventies and eighties. In 1979, at the invitation of Greg Gatenby, he gave his first public reading at Toronto's Harbourfront, reading from an early draft of *A Time for Judas* — an excerpt that included a discussion between a writer and an editor of apocryphal Christian scrolls.

The professional efflorescence of the sixties and seventies was matched by a thoroughly happy homelife. As always, Callaghan enjoyed his family, which continued to sustain him both personally and professionally. Until the late sixties, Loretto, his lifelong companion, continued to read, critique, and proofread his manuscripts; and both travelled frequently to New York, where they enjoyed not only the publishers' parties and literary circuit, but also the restaurants, galleries, and theatres.

Throughout his life Callaghan was especially close to his two sons, Barry and Michael, who were, by this point, already successful in their chosen professions. The elder son, Michael, worked as an executive with the McLaren Advertising Agency, and, like his grandfather, Thomas, became active on behalf of the Ontario Liberals. Barry shared a unique bond with his father: like Morley, he had worked as a part-time reporter in the late fifties and early sixties, and from 1965 onwards, has lived a variety of literary careers. Barry has been a literary editor for the Toronto *Telegram*; a prizewinning journalist; a controversial

FIGURE 8

Callaghan in uncharacteristic splendour:
receiving the Royal Bank Award in 1970.

television host and producer for CBC Television (in 1976 he was briefly imprisoned in South Africa during the filming of *The White Lager*); an interviewer, meeting such personalities as Golda Meir and King Hussein; a professor of English at Atkinson College, York University; the editor of *Exile*, a literary magazine which he founded in 1972 (it would later publish some of Callaghan's drafts of *The Enchanted Pimp* and *Our Lady of the Snows*); and publisher of Exile Editions. A noted poet and short-story writer, Barry Callaghan has also written, amongst others, *The Hogg Poems and Drawings* (1978) and *The Black Queen Stories* (1982).

Not only would father and son critique each other's work — with Barry helping in the revisions of *Season of the Witch* — but through Barry, Callaghan would enjoy the company of painters, artists, and musicians in his later years. Together they would visit late-night clubs in downtown Toronto and New York, listening to Barry's friends, the blues musicians Sonny Terry and Brownie McGee.

Callaghan's last quarter-century, in other words, was by no means a time of retirement slumber. If anything, it was a period of extraordinary renaissance. From 1963 until his death in 1990, Callaghan continued to work as a novelist, journalist, and play-wright, while making numerous diversions into film, television, and radio work. What is perhaps most striking is that Callaghan's abrasive individualism, his truly antagonistic attitude to all things official, increased rather than decreased as he got older. At a time when most men would doze quietly by the fire, Callaghan became more outspoken, more contrarian, more gad-flyish. Like his own Eugene Shore in *A Fine and Private Place*, he now truly despised and wrote against "[a]ll the big law-and-order men. . . . Cops of the courts, cops of the church, political cops. Society's cops" (88).

As the sixties progressed, and as Callaghan slowly but surely became one of Canada's grand old men of writing, he began to develop what might be called a critical nostalgia, a ficto-critical reappraisal of his life and writing. He began, not simply to

rewrite old stories and novels, but to refigure previously published fictions, interviews, and journalism into new fictional
contexts. He now initiated what would become the last phase in
his literary and personal development, a phase marked by a
curiously introspective, almost compulsive retrospection of his
writing career.

To be sure, the writing still had that combative flavour — the
later work is anything but muted in its intellectual, political,
and philosophical positioning — but through continual self-
reference, through frequent reappraisals of his past work,
Callaghan now, more than ever, sought to distinguish himself
from his origins: from European, American, and Canadian influences. As Callaghan grew older, he would begin a series of books
that continuously looked back in anger and amusement, that
repeatedly struggled to counterdevelop a fictional language of
his own, distinct from, yet contingent upon, traditional and
contemporary practices. This metafictional turn would continue throughout his seventies and eighties, reaching its apogee
in his last completed novel, the self-reflexively entitled *A Wild Old
Man on the Road*.

REWRITES AND REVELATIONS

Callaghan's self-reflexive practice and anarchistic attitudes are
evident in all his media work of the late sixties and seventies.
Again, he appeared as a wily and argumentative panellist on CBC
Radio's *Now I Ask You*; a tough reviewer, of Hemingway and
Fitzgerald to name but two, for *Saturday Night*, the *Telegram*, and
the *New York Times Book Review*; a journalist, writing articles for
both the *Telegram* and the *Tamarack Review*; a CBC Television
reporter, covering the murder of Pierre Laporte in October 1970.
In addition, while *More Joy in Heaven* was being serialized by
Melwyn Breen and Ron Weyman for CBC Television in 1964,
Callaghan wrote the critical essays "An Ocean Away," "The
Pleasures of Failure," and "The Imaginative Writer."

FIGURE 9

The elder novelist in 1978.

In these essays, Callaghan continued to berate the conservative and repressive nature of mainstream tastes and politics. As in his 1937 portrayal of the outlaw, Kip Caley, in *More Joy in Heaven*, he still championed the necessity of being true to oneself, of seeing the world through one's own eyes, not the authorized eyes of society. But alongside these critical attacks, Callaghan included ironic self-interrogation, initiating a meditative retrospective of the principles and practices of his own writerly career.

"An Ocean Away" is a critical watershed, for here Callaghan not only speaks simply and straightforwardly of his lifelong devotion to a North American idiom, but also of his own strategies for writerly independence:

By the time I came to think of English literature as the literature of another country, not my own, much of it had been ground into me. . . . When I showed some of my first stories to academic men highly trained in English literature [around 1923], I could see them turning up their noses. "A failure of language," one said to me; and feeling encouraged I said, "No, a failure on your part to understand the language." I had decided that language of feeling and perception, and even direct observation had to be the language of the people I wrote about, who did not belong in an English social structure at all. Under these circumstances my reading of the traditional English novelists was having a strange effect on me. The reading deepened my desire to write, and that was wonderful. But I was a young man looking for a master, sometimes thinking I had found one, and then walking out on him, impatient and irritated. ("An Ocean Away" 17)

Amidst the swirl of activity at this point in his life, Callaghan was inexorably drawn to his past work, incapable of resisting the need to reread, rewrite, and reevaluate the meanings of his life. One manifestation of this urge for retrospection was Callaghan's decision to narrate some of his early stories for CBC Radio's *Anthology* in 1967 and 1968. Over a two-year period he recorded more than forty of his best stories.

This critical self-reflexivity was also manifested when he began, as early as 1963, to rewrite a number of his earlier manuscripts. According to both Brandon Conron and David Latham, Callaghan began work in 1963 on a novel tentatively entitled "Thumbs Down on Julien Jones" — a novel set first in wartime New York and then at sea (Conron, *Morley Callaghan* [1966] xvi; Latham 24). According to Latham, Callaghan eventually abandoned this work-in-progress except for one episode — "The Meterman, Caliban, and Then Mr. Jones" — which was published as a short story in *Exile* in 1973 and adapted for the 1974 CBC Television production, *And Then Mr. Jones*. But the facts of the matter suggest a much more complex and elusive writerly development. As Callaghan began recasting his earlier screenplay, he also inaugurated a fascinating process of resurrection and revision that would entail an extraordinary amount of complex rewriting and new writing over the next twenty-two years.

After the publication of *That Summer in Paris* in 1963, Callaghan began to fossick through his early writings, seeking an initiatory spark of inspiration for a new novel. The existence of the 1942 NFB script — *Action Stations* — proves that Callaghan did in fact possess some older material with a "war-time setting . . . at sea" (Latham 24) — a setting that would reappear, in part, thirty-five years later in *Close to the Sun Again* (1977). But only in part. What seems to have happened is that in rethinking the NFB script, Callaghan certainly did recast it and begin to derive a novel tentatively called "Thumbs Down on Julien Jones" from it. But as he developed this new novel from his old filmic script, he also began, perhaps unknowingly, to lay the groundwork for a number of future works. This time Callaghan did not abandon the manuscript but began to divide the solitary filmic figure of "The Old Man" into two separate characters, and the plot into a framework for at least five different works. The process ran something like this.

One variation of "The Old Man" definitely became the urbanely debonair Ira Groome in *Close to the Sun Again*; likewise, the 1942 character of the bosun, who revives a half-drowned man, reappears in this 1977 novel. But the 1942 figure of "The Old Man" was also transferred to the unpublished 1963 novel manuscript, "Thumbs Down on Julien Jones." Callaghan later read four extracts from this manuscript in June 1970 on CBC Radio's *Anthology*. The story changes the figure of "The Old Man" into the nebulous and evil clubfooted pimp, Edmund J. Debuke, a fascinating dwarflike figure who mercilessly exploits a warm-hearted idiosyncratic prostitute named Ellen Delury. This broadcast version was then later adapted as the short story, "The Meterman, Caliban, and Then Mr. Jones," which appeared in *Exile* in 1973. A year later, Callaghan revised this short story into a play, "And Then Mr. Jones," which appeared on CBC Television's *The Play's the Thing* in January 1974.

Still not content, Callaghan returned to the "Meterman" story four years later, in 1978, a year after *Close to the Sun Again* appeared. He then revised and published it (alongside a reprint of *No Man's Meat*) as the novella, *The Enchanted Pimp*. In this version Debuke has become Debuque, and Ellen the Hungarian, Isis-like prostitute, Ilona Tomory. Apparently obsessed with the character of Ilona (who, in fact, recalls the character Annie Laurie in *The Many Colored Coat*), Callaghan then recast *The Enchanted Pimp* as the revised novella, "The Stepping Stone," which appeared in *Exile* in 1979. Six years later, unrepentant towards charges of shameless recycling, Callaghan carefully expanded virtually all of the previous versions of the "Meterman" story into the 1985 novel, *Our Lady of the Snows*.

The point of this long and contorted catalogue is that in the saga of Ilona Tomory and Edmund J. Debuque, Callaghan not only meticulously crystallized two of his most recurrent figures — the criminal and the saintly prostitute — but he also returned to a number of themes that had dominated his entire *oeuvre*. This saga contains, in almost pristine form, such grand themes as personal versus public justice; the redemptive nature of erotic love; the salvation of a sacred humanism unfettered by institutionalized religious scruples. Ilona is the virtual embodiment of all Callaghan's rejuvenating women: she is also, without doubt, the fictionalized idealization of his own beloved, Loretto Dee. What Callaghan was doing in this vast series of rewritings, in other words, was drawing together the multiple strands of his entire life, drawing the past into one coherent, golden present.

As Callaghan set about this grand revision, he simultaneously produced a series of novels that also constituted a personal retrospective. As is well known, *A Fine and Private Place* puckishly casts Callaghan himself as the elderly novelist, Eugene Shore, "the guy who wrote the book about the two hookers and the priest" (94). *Season of the Witch* is a revision of "Going Home," the earlier 1940s adaptation of *They Shall Inherit the Earth*; *A Time for Judas* likewise resurrects Callaghan's past journalism and literary criticism. For example, in *A Time for Judas* Philo records Simon's belief that "in the long run a man had only his own self-respect to fall back on" (39) — this is a virtual paraphrase of Callaghan's 1958 interview with Robert Weaver, his 1973 interview with Donald Cameron, and his critical articles, "Novelist" and "The Pleasures of Failure." In effect, what we see in this last phase of Callaghan's career is the elder artist undergoing a period of solitude, a period of critical recapitulation and theoretical reappraisal.

LOSS AND RETROSPECTION

Amidst the professional successes of his last thirty years, time and events began to take their toll on the aging novelist. Though Callaghan pummelled a burglar and chased him from his property when he was in his mid-seventies, he nonetheless began to feel the inevitable chill of decrepitude. Friends began to die in quick succession: Hemingway in 1961, Nathan Asch in 1964, Josephine Herbst in 1969. Likewise, the Toronto of his youth was changing rapidly: gone were the safe late-night walks with Nicky, his beloved poodle; gone were the convivial outings in the city.

FIGURE 10

Morley Callaghan/Eugene Shore with his prized poodle,
Nicky, walking across the Bloor Street Viaduct.

Highrises dominated the once quiet Rosedale. Downtown was punctuated with racist conflicts, shootings, and increased violent crime, events that worked their way into *A Fine and Private Place*.

By far most devastating for Morley and his family, amidst this gradual decline of their city and circle of friends, was Loretto's painful physical deterioration which began in the late 1960s. Vivacious and warm, Loretto had had an almost pre-Raphaelite beauty and sensitivity, as well as a quiet intelligence that intuitively grasped the nature of people or events. In 1992, friends still recalled how she had been Callaghan's main emotional stalwart — a beautiful, warm woman who was his supporter, friend, critic, lover, and wife. The two were by no means cripplingly dependent on each other; on the contrary, the Callaghan marriage was one of mutual intellectual respect, emotional passion, and human joy. As one friend of the family remarked, Loretto, more often than not, was *the* woman in Callaghan's novels.

But in the late sixties she began to suffer the effects of tic douloureux syndrome, a disease of the nervous system that causes painful paralysis of the facial nerves. Subsequently, in the mid-seventies, she suffered a horrifying series of pacemaker failures which left her severely debilitated. Though in considerable pain, she was still, in 1983, alert, engaged, and exquisitely interested in the world around her. She was delighted when Callaghan, at the age of eighty, won the 1983 Booksellers' "Author of the Year" award for *A Time for Judas*. But the delight was short-lived; Loretto died the next year, in 1984. Throughout her illness, Callaghan had been the principal caregiver. Her passing left him resigned, saddened, and empty — but still resolutely independent.

Following Loretto's death, Callaghan obstinately refused to live with either son, preferring to remain alone in the rambling, beautiful home on Dale Avenue in Rosedale. He was now eighty-one, widowed, and in declining health. For a number of years he had suffered a deterioration of the upper vertebrae which caused him excruciating headaches, and which accounted for his slight

FIGURE 11

With Loretto on his 80th birthday, 22 February 1983.

stoop in later years. But as photographs from this period suggest, he retained an impish vivacity, a sardonic sense of humour, and a virtually irrepressible engagement with life — an engagement which new friends like Margaret Atwood and Graeme Gibson found irresistible in their now frequent visits to Dale Avenue. In 1985 Callaghan collaborated with his son, Barry, in the publication of *The Lost and Found Stories of Morley Callaghan*, a collection of previously published but unanthologized short stories. In 1987, he travelled again to his beloved Paris, where he appeared in a CBC Television documentary, *First Person Singular*, reminiscing about his activities in the twenties.

In 1986 he also began work on his last published novel, the incomparable *A Wild Old Man on the Road*. Vintage Callaghan, the book traces the adventures of Mark Didion, who, discovering his dead father's long-secreted diary, retraces his father's Parisian experiences of the twenties. With multiple echoes of *That Summer in Paris* and *A Fine and Private Place*, Mark meets the enigmatic Jeremy Monk, an old revolutionary writer who "was a revered cult figure concerned only with truthful reporting" (5). As Monk progressively begins to "get religion," Mark becomes obsessed with Monk's mysterious young wife, Cretia Sampari. By engaging with both, he travels the long road of experience and comes to grips with birth, sex, death, truth, betrayal, loyalty, art, literature — all conventional Callaghan ambiguities.

The book is punctuated with acerbic swipes at avant-garde writing; ironic nonreminiscences of Joyce and Hemingway; vitalist pleas to see life "for the first and the only time" (48); naïve wonderment over the mysteries of the individual; and self-justifying defences of "a good straightforward style" (8). The novel has the allure of a fairy tale, an almost elemental mystique that pervades language, plot, and character. Warts and all, the novel is a critical retrospective foregrounding many of Callaghan's characteristic reflexes, sustaining and interrogating much of his thought and writing of the past sixty years.

FIGURE 12

Morley and Barry Callaghan in 1988:
their planned memoirs were never started.

FIGURE 13

Callaghan outside 20 Dale Avenue.

CONCLUSION: AGAINST THE GRAIN

Morley Callaghan continued working until the very end of his life. Although he broke his hip in a fall in the late eighties and began to suffer the general decline of age, he began a novella in 1988 with the aid of his amanuensis and typist, Dagmar Novak. It had the working title, "In the Park," and was, according to Barry Callaghan, "almost finished" by 1990. Callaghan planned to dictate his memoirs to Barry over the summer of 1990, to write, as it were, the sequel to *That Summer in Paris* and *A Wild Old Man on the Road*. But his health declined severely, and by July he was admitted to hospital where he underwent surgery for internal bleeding.

On 25 August 1990, a Saturday, Canada's grand old man of letters died peacefully in his sleep, with his sons, Barry and Michael, at his bedside. Fittingly, and at his own request, Callaghan had a Roman Catholic burial service at St. Michael's Cathedral in downtown Toronto. It was attended, not only by writers and publishers, friends and family, but also by "members" of his personal circus-temple: boxers and cardinals, priests and hoods, artists and comedians, politicians and police.

What is perhaps an ironic tribute to Callaghan's perpetual antagonism to mainstream Canadian life and thought is the fact that his death was reported by Toronto's *Globe and Mail*, not on the front page, but as a profile by Marilyn Powell in the arts section. To many Canadian writers this decision constituted a slight of the highest order: as Timothy Findley wrote in his letter to the editor, the *Globe*'s "failure . . . to find Mr. Callaghan's death newsworthy" was a failure to acknowledge that he was not only "a major figure in the Canadian literary landscape," but "a major figure in the literary landscape of the twentieth century." True to form, Callaghan's death, like his life, ran against the popular grain, against what Findley described as "the wasteland of anti-cultural, money-oriented politics. . . ."

But somehow, ruefully, that decision to remove Callaghan safely to the "less newsworthy" section of the public record

FIGURE 14

Morley Callaghan at home in Rosedale, 1988.

FIGURE 15

"The most unjustly neglected novelist in the English-speaking world."

seems oddly appropriate. As Brandon Conron remarked, Callaghan observed throughout his life and writing an "unwritten charter of responsibilities" (Personal interview 1991) — a charter that followed, not the impoverished pathways of public officialdom, but the contours of the human heart and mind, the intricacies of anarchistic freedom and struggle.

As Callaghan meditated almost thirty years earlier in *That Summer in Paris*, "Does the dolphin or the rose flourish with an eye on eternity?" On the contrary, he continued, "Our job . . . [was] to realize all our possibilities here on earth, and hope we would always be so interested, so willing to lose ourselves in the fullness of living, and so hopeful that we would never ask why we were on this earth" (110–11). Throughout his life, in his happy but critical acceptance of reality, Morley Callaghan sustained this vitalist desire, this anarchic refusal of givens. In the process he created a body of writing that challenged — and still challenges — readers. His writing still mystifies, puzzles, irritates, and confounds. Most importantly, it still runs against the grain.

NOTES

1 In an undated letter to Hemingway, Callaghan says, " 'Tis true you read the long one once, but it has been rewritten, broken up, and, I think, made a good deal better. If you'll read it as a new story I think you'll agree with me. In my search for a title for the long story: I came across nothing I like so well as a phrase taken from a poesy of yours. 'Yesterday's Tribune is gone along with youth.' If you would sanction it, I would like to call the story 'Along with Youth' " (Letter to Hemingway, [Autumn 1925]). See *That Summer in Paris* (35) and Robert Weaver's interview with Callaghan ("Talk" 12), where Callaghan recounts the rejection of the story by Ford Madox Ford.

2 One of the most telling indicators of the anxiety underlying their obviously mutual admiration can be detected in Callaghan's early review of Hemingway's *In Our Time* and *The Torrents of Spring*, "Introducing Ernest Hemingway." The essay suggests that each writer read in the other's work what he most wanted (or needed) to achieve in his own. Callaghan's review is unstinting in its praise of Hemingway as having produced "the best short stories coming from an American today" (7). In fact, Callaghan praises those very qualities that he was beginning to formulate as his own artistic ideals. Hemingway's writing, Callaghan argues, is marked by "a direct simplicity and earthy flavor quite foreign to the King's English and the literary language of professors, which makes it a spoken language with a feeling for the natural rhythms that are colloquial" (7). Interestingly, while Callaghan celebrates the Fieldingesque ebullience of Hemingway's satire of Anderson's *Dark Laughter*, he ends his review in virtually identical fashion to his earlier letter to Hemingway, praising Anderson's work as "distinguished" (8). See also "An Ocean Away," where Callaghan restates many of these principles with the wisdom of hindsight.

3 Chapter two is a revision of "The Novice" which appeared in the *Canadian Magazine* Mar. 1930: 11+; chapter twelve is a revision of "The Young Priest" which appeared in the *New Yorker* Sept. 1930: 24–27.

4 I am indebted here to Professor William James's essay, "The Ambiguities of Love in Morley Callaghan's *Such Is My Beloved*," from which I have borrowed extensively. I thank Professor James for his kind permission to read the original manuscript of this article. See also John J. O'Connor's excellent appraisal, "Fraternal Twins: The Impact of Jacques Maritain on Callaghan and Charbonneau."

5 The subject matter of *Going Home* — the limitations of the legal system and the need for private resolutions to public immorality — would reappear in various versions in *The Loved and the Lost* (1951), *The Many Colored Coat*

(1960), and *A Fine and Private Place* (1975), all of which contain distinctly theatrical sequences. In addition, George and his flute-playing search for truth from "Just Ask for George," would become Arthur Tyndall and his flute in *The Varsity Story* (1948); likewise, the rag-bag neo-Brechtian cast of prostitutes, boxers, and bums of "Just Ask for George" would continue to populate Callaghan's novels of the fifties and sixties.

6 For a detailed account of Callaghan's journalistic output at this time, see Judith Kendle's "Morley Callaghan: An Annotated Bibliography," and her excellent bibliographical essay, "Callaghan as Columnist, 1940–48."

7 As Judith Kendle has pointed out, "Callaghan describes his contribution to the film as a minor one, confined simply to 'touching up' the script" ("Morley Callaghan: An Annotated Bibliography" 52). A revised version of *Hot Ice* for Sterling Films appeared in 1948, but neither Callaghan's name, nor Jacoby's, is mentioned in the credits.

8 "Just Ask for George" was never produced in New York and had to wait until 1949 when it was directed by Mavor Moore and retitled *To Tell the Truth*. It was first staged at the Royal Ontario Museum Theatre by the New Play Society from 14 to 22 January 1949; soon after it was moved and staged at the Royal Alexandra Theatre, again by the New Play Society. The play was a resounding financial and critical success, with Don Harron in the role of George, Lloyd Bochner as the unscrupulous Taylor, Dianne Foster as Dini, E.M. Margolese as Shultz, and John Sullivan as the promoter, Henderson. In April 1949, J.K. Thomas wrote in the *National Home Monthly*, "Callaghan is a moralist — unlike Hemingway, and he is more profound than Saroyan, who inevitably ends in sentimentalism. . . . Callaghan writes with compassion, understanding and perception" (35). Though Thomas mentions that the play is to be produced on Broadway with James Stewart and Margaret Sullivan in the leading roles, I have been unable to verify any American production. However, Mavor Moore himself returned to the play later the same year: he adapted the script for radio broadcast, directed by Esse W. Ljungh, on 25 May 1949 on CBC *Wednesday Night*. Three years later Silvio Marizzano directed the play for television; it was broadcast on 23 October 1952 on *CBC Theatre*.

9 Callaghan waited ten years for *Going Home* to be produced. Finally, under the direction of Mavor Moore, the play was staged by the New Play Society at the Royal Ontario Museum Theatre from 24 March until 1 April 1950. The cast included Don Harron, Robert Christie, Gerry Sarracini, and Tony Robbins. After the stage production, Moore adapted the script for a CBC Radio broadcast. Later, under the direction of Michael Mawson in 1976, Wenjak Theatre produced the play for the Peterborough Summer Theatre Festival under the title *Season of the Witch*. In scripting this version, Callaghan was aided by his son, Barry; among other things, they introduced different character names. *Season of the Witch* was edited by Barry Callaghan and published by Exile Editions in Toronto in 1976.

CHRONOLOGY

1903   Edward Morley Callaghan born on 22 February in Toronto, the second son of Roman Catholic parents of Irish-Welsh descent: Thomas Callaghan (b. 1872, Wales) and Mary Dewan (b. 1870, Collingwood, Ontario).

1909–21   Attends Withrow Public School and Riverdale Collegiate. During high school he begins reading contemporary American writers who would influence his style and themes. Publishes his first article, "A Windy Corner at Yonge-Albert," in the Toronto *Star Weekly* during his final year at Riverdale.

1921–25   Attends St. Michael's College, University of Toronto. Opts for a general arts degree, reading widely in English, French, philosophy, economics, and geology; enjoys debating, baseball, hockey, and boxing. In 1923 begins his first of four summer jobs as a junior reporter for the Toronto *Star Weekly* where he becomes friends with Ernest Hemingway. Meets Loretto Dee at a school dance in 1924. Callaghan has already begun to write short stories.

1925–28   Attends Osgoode Hall Law School and articles with Joseph Sedgwick in whose office he begins "An Autumn Penitent." Corresponds with Hemingway in Paris, sending stories for circulation among the little magazines. Publishes "A Girl with Ambition" in 1926 in the Paris magazine, *This Quarter*; in the same year begins *Strange Fugitive*, his first novel. Visits New York and meets Nathan Asch, Ford Madox Ford, Katherine Ann Porter, Allen Tate, Josephine Herbst, and William

Carlos Williams. With his boyhood friend, Art Kent, Callaghan opens the Viking Lending Library in 1926; meets Raymond Knister. Completes his law degree in 1928. Meets Max Perkins of Scribner's in New York, who publishes *Strange Fugitive* in 1928 and commissions Callaghan's first collection of short stories, *A Native Argosy*. Callaghan begins to write literary reviews for *Saturday Night*.

1929   A major transitional period. Marries Loretto Florence Dee, daughter of Joseph Dee and Catherine Hamlin, on 16 April in Toronto. They travel together to New York and then to Paris, where they remain until late September. The Callaghans socialize with Hemingway, F. Scott Fitzgerald, James Joyce, Edward Titus, and Robert McAlmon. Callaghan completes a novel, *It's Never Over*, and a novella, *No Man's Meat*. He returns to Toronto via Dublin and New York. *A Native Argosy* is published.

1930–32   Supports himself by writing stories for such magazines as *Atlantic Monthly*, *Esquire*, and the *New Yorker*. Shuttles back and forth for eight months in 1930 between a farmhouse in Pennsylvania and a hotel in New York City before taking up permanent residence in Toronto. His first son, Michael Burke, is born on 20 November 1931. Publishes *It's Never Over* in 1930; *No Man's Meat* in 1931; and *A Broken Journey* in 1932.

1933–37   In 1933 becomes friends with Catholic philosopher Jacques Maritain, who begins a six-year contact with the Pontifical Institute of Medieval Studies at the University of Toronto. Callaghan lives in New York for six months during 1936. His second son, Barry Morley Joseph, is born on 5 July 1937. Publishes four major books in four years: *Such Is My Beloved* in 1934; *They Shall Inherit the Earth* in 1935 (banned for its "immorality" by the Toronto Public Library); *Now That April's Here and Other Stories* in 1936; and *More Joy in Heaven* in 1937.

1938–47　A "dark period" of Callaghan's life, yet one of feverish journalistic activity. Stops writing novels and stories and begins a variety of jobs: works as a playwright in 1939, writing "Just Ask for George" and "Turn Again Home"; in 1940 joins the Civil Liberties Union and becomes a sports columnist and regular contributor for *New World Illustrated* until 1948; in 1942 spends the summer aboard a Royal Canadian Navy corvette and writes a screenplay for the National Film Board of Canada to be directed by Joris Ivens; from 1943 until 1947 appears on CBC Radio's *Of Things to Come* and *Beat the Champs*. In 1946 his only brother, Burke, dies at the age of 44. Resumes writing stories in 1947.

1948　Callaghan experiences a resurgence of literary creativity: he begins one of his finest novels, *The Loved and the Lost*; expands and publishes a 1947 short story as the novel, *Luke Baldwin's Vow*; and publishes, on behalf of the University of Toronto's fund-raising campaign, *The Varsity Story*. Callaghan's father dies at age 76.

1950–55　Mother dies in 1950 at the age of 80. Callaghan is still active with the CBC as a radio host on *Now I Ask You*, and as a guest panellist on the television show *Fighting Words*. In 1952 moves with family to permanent residence at 20 Dale Avenue in Toronto. Begins a new novel-writing phase: publishes *The Loved and the Lost* in 1951 which wins the Governor General's Award for Fiction; wins the 1955 *Maclean's* Magazine Award for his short novel "The Man with the Coat," which he later expands and revises to become *The Many Colored Coat*.

1957–60　American critic Edmund Wilson visits Callaghan in Toronto in 1957. In 1958 Callaghan travels to Rome for the *Star Weekly* to cover the Pope's death; this experience forms the basis for his later novel, *A Passion in Rome*. In 1960 Wilson publishes his famous essay "Morley Callaghan of Toronto," describing Callaghan as "the most unjustly neglected novelist in the English-speaking world." Publishes *Morley Callaghan's Stories*, a collection of his own favourites, in 1959, and *The Many Colored Coat* in 1960. Receives the Lorne Pierce Medal in 1960 for his contribution to Canadian literature.

1961   Publishes *A Passion in Rome*. Receives the City of Toronto Civic Award of Merit.

1963   *That Summer in Paris*, Callaghan's memoir tracing his relationship with Ernest Hemingway and F. Scott Fitzgerald during the summer of 1929, is published; the book articulates his personal artistic credo. Begins "Thumbs Down on Julien Jones" which he will eventually rework and recast into a variety of stories and books.

1964–66   Writes "An Ocean Away," a short memoir about his writing experiences, for the *Times Literary Supplement* in 1964. A six-part serialization of *More Joy in Heaven* is broadcast in 1964 on CBC Television. Receives an honorary LL.D. from the University of Western Ontario in 1965 and, in 1966, an honorary D.Litt. from the University of Toronto and the Canada Council Medal.

1967   Rejects an offer of the Order of Canada Medal as a second-class honour inferior to the Companion Medal. Begins a series of readings from his short stories for CBC Radio's *Anthology*.

1970   Begins a series of talks for CBC *Anthology*'s monthly discussion series, "Books and Bookmen," which he will continue until 1983. Awarded the $15,000 Molson Prize in March and the $50,000 Royal Bank Award in June. Reads excerpts from "Thumbs Down on Julien Jones" on *Anthology* in June. Does television reports for CBC *Weekend* in October on the FLQ Pierre Laporte kidnapping and the War Measures Act.

1972   Writer-in-residence at the University of Windsor. Works on "In the Dark and Light of Lisa," which he will later develop into *A Fine and Private Place*.

1973   Awarded a D. Litt. from the University of Windsor. CBC televises a two-hour remake of *More Joy in Heaven*. Narrates and introduces twenty stories for a CBC cassette series, *Callaghan Stories*. *An Autumn Penitent* is republished.

1974   CBC Television production of "The Meterman, Caliban, and Then Mr. Jones" is adapted from the abandoned novel, "Thumbs Down on Julien Jones." *Winter*, with photos by John de Visser, is published.

1975–76   *A Fine and Private Place* is published in 1975. Adapts *They Shall Inherit the Earth* as a play, *Season of the Witch*, which is performed at the 1976 Peterborough Summer Festival and published the same year.

1977–78   *Close to the Sun Again* published in 1977; *No Man's Meat & The Enchanted Pimp* in 1978.

1979   At 76, gives his first public reading — from a draft of *A Time for Judas* — at Toronto's Harbourfront. "From the Stepping Stone" appears in *Exile*.

1980–85   Symposium devoted to his work is held at the University of Ottawa in 1980. Appointed Companion of the Order of Canada in 1982. In 1983 publishes *A Time for Judas*, which wins him the "Author of the Year" award from the Canadian Booksellers Association. Loretto Callaghan dies in 1984. *Our Lady of the Snows*, a reworking of *The Enchanted Pimp*, and *The Lost and Found Stories of Morley Callaghan* are published in 1985.

1986   Begins work on *A Wild Old Man on the Road*.

1987   CBC Television documentary, *First Person Singular*, is produced, with Callaghan returning to the scenes of his 1929 summer in Paris.

1988   Publishes *A Wild Old Man on the Road*, his last completed novel.

1989   Plans to dictate his memoirs to his son, Barry, are cancelled due to illness.

1990   Dies in hospital at the age of 87 on 25 August, leaving behind an unfinished novella, "In the Park." Roman Catholic funeral service held on 29 August at St.

Michael's Cathedral in Toronto. Major obituary in the *New York Times*. Toronto's *Globe and Mail* decides against front-page coverage; Timothy Findley protests this unpardonable slight to "a major figure in the literary landscape of the twentieth century."

WORKS CONSULTED

[*Note:* Although Callaghan rarely dated his letters by year, contextual remarks, internal references, and postmarks provide relatively reliable evidence for the dates ascribed herein. When the date of a letter is provisional, it is indicated both in the text and below within brackets.]

Baker, Carlos. *Ernest Hemingway: A Life Story.* New York: Scribner's, 1969.

——— , ed. *Ernest Hemingway: Selected Letters, 1917–1961.* New York: Scribner's, 1981.

Callaghan, Barry. Personal interviews. 1992.

Callaghan, Loretto. Letter to Peggy Brown. 8 May 1951. E.K. Brown Papers. National Archives of Canada, Ottawa.

——— . Letter to Josephine Herbst. [Dec. 1943]. Yale Collection of American Literature.

Callaghan, Morley. "Action Stations." Unpublished typescript. National Film Board of Canada Archives, Montreal.

——— . *Close to the Sun Again.* Toronto: Macmillan, 1977.

——— . *A Fine and Private Place.* Toronto: Macmillan, 1975.

——— . "The Imaginative Writer." *Tamarack Review* 41 (1966): 5–11.

——— . Interview. *Lifetime.* CTV Productions. 15 Jan. 1985.

——— . "Into the Dream World." Rev. of *Finnegans Wake*, by James Joyce. *Saturday Night* May 1939: 21.

——— . "Introducing Ernest Hemingway." Rev. of *In Our Time* and *The Torrents of Spring*, by Ernest Hemingway. *Saturday Night* Aug. 1926: 7–8.

——— . Letter to Nathan Asch. [1926–27]. Nathan Asch Papers. Dacus Library, Winthrop College, South Carolina.

——— . Letter to John Grierson. 17 Aug. [1942]. National Film Board of Canada Archives, Montreal.

———. Letter to Ernest Hemingway. [Autumn 1925]. Ernest Hemingway Papers.

———. Letter to Ernest Hemingway. 11 Oct. [1925]. Ernest Hemingway Papers.

———. Letter to Ernest Hemingway. 26 Apr. [1926]. Ernest Hemingway Papers.

———. Letter to Ernest Hemingway. 29 Apr. [1926]. Ernest Hemingway Papers.

———. Letter to Ernest Hemingway. 25 June [1926]. Ernest Hemingway Papers.

———. Letter to Ernest Hemingway. 12 Aug. [1926]. Ernest Hemingway Papers.

———. Letter to Ernest Hemingway. 22 Oct. [1926]. Ernest Hemingway Papers.

———. Letter to Ernest Hemingway. 27 Oct. [1926]. Ernest Hemingway Papers.

———. Letter to Ernest Hemingway. 7 Nov. [1926]. Ernest Hemingway Papers.

———. Letter to Ernest Hemingway. 8 Mar. [1927]. Ernest Hemingway Papers.

———. Letter to Josephine Herbst. 20 Mar. [1930]. Yale Collection of American Literature.

———. Letter to Josephine Herbst. 10 Feb. [1936]. Yale Collection of American Literature.

———. Letter to Josephine Herbst. 20 Jan. [1948]. Yale Collection of American Literature.

———. Letter to Josephine Herbst. [Dec. 1949]. Yale Collection of American Literature.

———. Letter to Josephine Herbst. [1960–61]. Yale Collection of American Literature.

———. Letter to Raymond Knister. [1928]. Raymond Knister Papers.

———. Letter to Raymond Knister. 15 Aug. 1928. Raymond Knister Papers.

———. Letter to Elizabeth McAfee. 8 May [1940]. Yale Collection of American Literature.

———. Letter to Max Perkins. [1929]. Charles Scribner's Publishing Archives.

———. Letter to Max Perkins. 20 Oct. [1931]. Charles Scribner's

Publishing Archives.

——— . Letter to Max Perkins. 29 May [1932]. Charles Scribner's Publishing Archives.

——— . Letter to Max Perkins. 14 June [1932]. Charles Scribner's Publishing Archives.

——— . Letter to Max Perkins. 14 June [1933]. Charles Scribner's Publishing Archives.

——— . Letter to Max Perkins. 3 Sept. [1933]. Charles Scribner's Publishing Archives.

——— . Letter to Max Perkins. 18 Dec. [1933]. Charles Scribner's Publishing Archives.

——— . Letter to Max Perkins. 11 Jan. [1934]. Charles Scribner's Publishing Archives.

——— . Letter to Max Perkins. 10 Sept. [1934]. Charles Scribner's Publishing Archives.

——— . Letter to Ezra Pound. [1926]. Yale Collection of American Literature.

——— . "Looking At Native Prose." *Saturday Night* Dec. 1928: 3.

——— . *Luke Baldwin's Vow.* Toronto: Winston, 1948.

——— . "Novelist." Canadian Writer's Conference. *Writing in Canada: Proceedings of the Canadian Writers' Conference, Queen's University, 28–31 July, 1955.* Ed. George Whalley. Toronto: Macmillan, 1957. 24–32.

——— . "An Ocean Away." 1964. *Morley Callaghan.* Conron 17–23.

——— . "The Past Quarter Century." *Maclean's* 15 Mar. 1936: 36, 38.

——— . Personal interview. 15 Jan. 1985.

——— . "The Pleasures of Failure." *Maclean's* 6 Mar. 1965: 12+.

——— . "The Plight of Canadian Fiction." *University of Toronto Quarterly* 7 (1938): 152–61.

——— . "Radical 'Bill' Foster Urges Labor Revolt." *Toronto Daily Star* 7 Aug. 1923: 5.

——— . *Strange Fugitive.* New York: Scribner's, 1928.

——— . *Such Is My Beloved.* New York: Scribner's, 1934.

——— . "A Talk with Morley Callaghan." With Robert Weaver. *Tamarack Review* 7 (1958): 3–29.

——— . *That Summer in Paris: Memories of Tangled Friendships with Hemingway, Fitzgerald, and Some Others.* Toronto: Macmillan, 1963.

——— . "There Are Gurus in the Woodwork." With Donald Cameron. *Conversations with Canadian Novelists: Part Two*. Toronto: Macmillan, 1973. 17–33.

——. *A Time for Judas*. Toronto: Macmillan, 1983.

——. *The Varsity Story*. Toronto: Macmillan, 1948.

——. "Where I Stand on Spain." *New Frontier* 8 (1936): 14.

——. "Why Single Out Sex as the Only Real Road to Sin?" *Maclean's* 2 Jan. 1960: 6+.

——. *A Wild Old Man on the Road*. Toronto: Stoddart, 1988.

——. "A Windy Corner at Yonge-Albert." *Toronto Star Weekly* 6 Aug. 1921: 17.

——. "Wipe Out Craft Unionism, States 'Most Dangerous Red.'" *Toronto Daily Star* 7 Aug. 1923: 8.

Charles Scribner's Publishing Archives. Series: Author file 1. Box 29, folder: Callaghan, Morley E. Princeton University Library, Princeton.

Colum, Mary. "The Psychopathic Novel." Conron 47–54.

Conron, Brandon. *Morley Callaghan*. New York: Twayne, 1966.

——, ed. *Morley Callaghan*. Critical Views on Canadian Writers. Toronto: McGraw, 1975.

——. Personal interviews. 12 and 28 Nov. 1991.

Daniels, Jonathan. "Night of the Soul." Conron 40–41.

Ernest Hemingway Papers. John Fitzgerald Kennedy Library, Boston.

Findley, Timothy. Letter. *Globe and Mail* 8 Sept. 1990: D7.

First Person Singular. Prod. Terence Macartney-Filgate. Narr. R.H. Thompson. CBC Television, Toronto. 26 Mar. 1987.

Globe [Toronto] 23 Feb. 1903: 1.

Herbst, Josephine. Letter to Morley Callaghan. 28 Dec. [1949]. Yale Collection of American Literature.

James, William. "The Ambiguities of Love in Morley Callaghan's *Such Is My Beloved*." *Canadian Literature* 138/139 (1993): 35–51.

Kendle, Judith. "Callaghan as Columnist, 1940–48." *Canadian Literature* 82 (1979): 6–20.

——. "Morley Callaghan: An Annotated Bibliography." *The Annotated Bibliography of Canada's Major Authors*. Ed. Robert Lecker and Jack David. Vol. 5. Toronto: ECW, 1984. 13–177. 8 vols. to date. 1979– .

Klenman, Norman. Letter to the author. 19 May 1991.

Latham, David. "A Callaghan Log." *Journal of Canadian Studies* 15

(1980): 18–29.

Lemon, James. *Toronto since 1918*. Toronto: Lorimer, 1985.

Maritain, Jacques. *Existence and the Existent*. Trans. Lewis Galantiere and Gerald B. Phelan. New York: Pantheon, 1948.

——. *An Introduction to Philosophy*. Trans. E.I. Watkin. London: Sheed, 1930.

——. *The Rights of Man and Natural Law*. Trans. Doris C. Anson. New York: Gordian, 1971.

——. *True Humanism*. Trans. M.R. Adamson. New York: Scribner's, 1938.

McPherson, Hugo. "The Two Worlds of Morley Callaghan." Conron [1975] 60–73.

O'Connor, John. "Fraternal Twins: The Impact of Jacques Maritain on Callaghan and Charbonneau." *Mosaic* 14 (1981): 145–63.

Pacey, Desmond. *Creative Writing in Canada: A Short History of English-Canadian Literature*. Toronto: Ryerson, 1952.

Patterson, Isabel. "Turns with a Bookworm." *New York Herald Tribune* 24 Nov. 1929: n. pag.

Raymond Knister Papers. William Ready Division of Archives and Research Collections, McMaster University, Hamilton.

Ross, Malcolm. *Our Sense of Identity: A Book of Canadian Essays*. Toronto: Ryerson, 1954.

Staines, David, ed. *The Callaghan Symposium*. 24–25 Apr. 1980. Re-Appraisals: Canadian Writers. Ottawa: U of Ottawa P, 1981.

Sutherland, Fraser. *The Style of Innocence: A Study of Hemingway and Callaghan*. Toronto: Clarke, 1972.

"T.C." "That Premier Majority — One." *Moon* 30 Aug. 1902: 195.

Thomas, J.K. "Mr. Callaghan Comes To Town." *National Home Monthly* Apr. 1949: 32–35.

Watt, Frank W. "Morley Callaghan as Thinker." *Dalhousie Review* 39 (1959): 305–13.

White, William, ed. *Ernest Hemingway, Dateline: Toronto*. New York: Scribner's, 1985.

Wilson, Edmund. "Morley Callaghan of Toronto." Conron 106–19.

Woodcock, George. "Lost Eurydice: The Novels of Callaghan." *Canadian Literature* 21 (1964): 21–35.

Yale Collection of American Literature. Beinecke Rare Book and Manuscript Library, Yale University, New Haven, Connecticut.